# The Infinite Resource

# William E. Halal, Editor

with

Raymond W. Smith, CEO of Bell Atlantic

David Walters, Former Governor of Oklahoma

William A. Owens, Former Vice Chairman,
   Joint Chiefs of Staff; President and COO,
   SAIC

Gerald H. Taylor, CEO, MCI Communications

Stephen Goldsmith, Mayor of Indianapolis

Robert Kuperman, CEO of Chiat/Day

Russell L. Ackoff, Chairman of INTERACT

Raymond E. Miles, Former Dean
   of the Haas School of Business,
   University of California

Gifford & Elizabeth Pinchot,
   Authors of *The Intelligent Organization*

Michael Malone, Coauthor of
   *The Virtual Corporation*

Jessica Lipnack and Jeffrey Stamps,
   Authors of *The Age of the Network*

Cases of Alcoa, Lufthansa, Chiat/Day, Koch,
   Novell, SAIC, and Telepad

# The Infinite Resource

## Creating and Leading the Knowledge Enterprise

Jossey-Bass Publishers
San Francisco

Substantial discounts on bulk quantities of Jossey-Bass books are available to corporations, professional associations, and other organizations. For details and discount information, contact the special sales department at Jossey-Bass Inc., Publishers (415) 433-1740; Fax (800) 605-2665.

For sales outside the United States, please contact your local Simon & Schuster International Office.

Jossey-Bass Web address: http://www.josseybass.com

 Manufactured in the United States of America on Lyons Falls Turin Book. This paper is acid-free and 100 percent totally chlorine-free.

**Library of Congress Cataloging-in-Publication Data**

The infinite resource: creating and managing the knowledge enterprise/
    William E. Halal with Raymond Smith.—1st ed.
        p.    cm.—(The Jossey-Bass business & management series)
    ISBN 0-7879-1015-5 (alk. paper)
    1. Knowledge management—Congresses. 2. Organizational change—
Congresses. 3. Organizational learning—Congresses. I. Halal,
William E. II. Smith, Raymond, 1937–  . III. Series.
HD30.2.I52    1998
658.4'06—dc21                                                97-33910

FIRST EDITION
*HB Printing*    10 9 8 7 6 5 4 3 2 1

The Jossey-Bass
Business & Management Series

# Contents

*To those pioneers of the Information Age, the extrepreneurial men and women who are hacking out the next frontier of civilization with little more than knowledge.*

# Acknowledgments

This book would not have been possible without the George Washington University conference, "Creating the New Organization," that produced this material. I want to thank all those who contributed to this event: David Fowler, the dean of our school who supported this undertaking and the subsequent book and CD-ROM; Barbara Maddox, director of our Office of Professional Development who planned and carried out the logistics; my assistant Mike Kull for his continuing efforts on my behalf; and many other colleagues who encouraged this endeavor. I am particularly grateful to Cedric Crocker and the staff at Jossey-Bass for their fine efforts in bringing this book to press. Special recognition is reserved for the executives, scholars, and consultants whose work forms the basis of this book. I hope they will feel I have treated their thoughts respectfully, and that I have enhanced what they have to say by organizing it into a broader conceptual framework.

# About the Editor

WILLIAM E. HALAL is Professor of Management at George Washington University in Washington, D.C. An authority on emerging technologies, strategic management, and institutional and economic change, he has conducted research and consulting projects for General Motors, IBM, AT&T, Blue Cross/Blue Shield, MCI, International Data Corporation, Japanese firms, the Saudi Arabian firm Petromin, and various governments.

Halal's publications have appeared in journals such as *California Management Review*, *Business in the Contemporary World*, *Academy of Management Executive*, *Human Relations*, *Systems & Cybernetics*, and *Technological Forecasting & Social Change*, as well as popular media such as the *New York Times*, *Christian Science Monitor*, *Advertising Age*, *New Portable MBA*, and *The Futurist*. His 1986 book *The New Capitalism* (Wiley) outlines the transition to a new system of business and economics for the Information Age, and his 1993 book *Internal Markets* (Wiley) describes how dynamic organizations are replacing the hierarchy with internal market economies. His recent book, *The New Management* (Berrett-Koehler, 1996), shows that the principles of democracy and enterprise are transforming organizations.

Halal has studied engineering, business and economics, and the social sciences at Purdue and Berkeley, and he held positions as an Air Force officer, aerospace engineer, and business manager. He serves on the advisory boards of the World Future Society and Sterling & Stone Publishers as well as several journals.

Halal's work has received prominent recognition. One paper, "Beyond the Profit-Motive," won the 1977 Mitchell Prize and an award of $10,000. In 1985 he was awarded the George Washington Honor Medal by the Freedoms Foundation at Valley Forge for excellence in the study of enterprise.

# The Infinite Resource

# Introduction

# The Economic Imperatives of Knowledge
## New Organizations for a New Era

### William E. Halal

Just a few years ago, most people would have laughed at the idea that business should focus on creating *knowledge*. Yet knowledge has come to dominate management attention recently as the Information Revolution rewires the corporation.

## Editor's Overview

The flowering of entrepreneurial organizations, collaborative alliances, and intelligent information systems can be insightfully understood as a watershed in economics: the discovery of powerful new principles for managing the boundless power of knowledge that drives creative enterprise—the *infinite resource*.

### The Flowering of Enterprise

Information technology (IT) created the world's first interconnected global markets at the start of this decade, thereby forcing big corporations such as IBM to dismantle their old hierarchies and encouraging myriad entrepreneurs to start new ventures everywhere. Now we celebrate entrepreneurial firms such as Asea Brown Boveri (ABB), which is composed of five thousand self-managed units interacting freely within an "internal market." Even the U.S. government is trying to become entrepreneurial.[1]

What is the meaning of this historic devolution of authority? To manage exploding complexity and constant change, executives are moving decision making downward to free up the skills, creativity, and vision of countless ordinary people. The role of leaders remains crucial, of course, but the big shift has been to release the knowledge lying dormant at the bottom of economies, and now it is electrifying business around the globe.

## The Birth of Economic Cooperation

We also witnessed a remarkable rush of collaboration as the benefits of alliances were discovered by all organizations—large and small, private and public, domestic and foreign. Microsoft dominates computer use worldwide through a complex coalition of alliances, forming an entire constellation of cooperating corporations.

Having fanned an information explosion by releasing the raw energy of free enterprise, alliances then harness it into productive exchanges as firms pool their technologies, markets, and competencies. In system terms, cooperation amplifies the flow of knowledge through this global network, with mounting gains in its velocity and value.

## The Integrating Role of Knowledge

And now a third force is emerging with still more power. The Information Revolution is accelerating a burst of activity in organizational learning, intelligent organizations, intellectual assets, and other exciting new concepts focusing directly on the creation and management of knowledge. Most companies now boast of having an intranet managed by a CIO, chief knowledge officer, or director of corporate learning.

In effect, CEOs are tracking the path of successful management to its ultimate source—the brain of the corporation and its central nervous system connecting diverse people and numerous units into a coordinated, creative whole. We see now that knowledge is the most strategic asset in enterprise, the source of all creativity, innovation, and economic value.

## Limited Only by Intelligence, Skill, and Imagination

The possibilities are truly unimaginable, especially because we do not yet really understand the mysterious, boundless quality of this unique form of power. Knowledge inhabits a more ethereal realm, with principles we are only now coming to grasp and purposes we can only imagine. Unlike other resources we are accustomed to, information is a fluid that constantly alters as it moves, increases when exchanged, and overflows boundaries.

In a following chapter, Raymond Smith, CEO of Bell Atlantic, describes this quality as the principle of loaves and fishes: "Unlike raw materials, knowledge can't be used up. The more you dispense, the more you generate." Or consider the much celebrated cloning of a sheep, the lovely Dolly. Does anyone really believe this knowledge can be restricted now?

Information is the infinite resource, as we shall soon see, because it represents a boundless supply of boundless power to manage a world of boundless potential. The meteoric rise of millions of entrepreneurs like Bill Gates and entire economies like South Korea illustrates that we have broken the bonds once holding humankind captive to a material world. All the normal obstacles remain, but I think it is now possible to accomplish almost anything. The possibilities are virtually infinite, and the only limits lie in our intelligence, skill, and imagination.

## The New Principles of Progress

But economics has been traditionally called "the dismal science." It was based on *limited* resources that *decrease* when shared to produce a world of *scarcity*. That's why information is revolutionary—it challenges everything we learned in the past.

This book brings together the views of prominent leaders in the trenches of the Information Revolution to examine the revolutionary new principles for managing knowledge. Here's a quick

*Is the "infinite" Resource Knowledge or I* [handwritten]

overview of these confusing but exciting management heresies that we will soon examine more fully.

> *Principle 1: Complexity Is Managed Through Freedom.* Success is no longer achieved by planning and control—but through entrepreneurial freedom among people at the bottom.

> *Principle 2: Cooperation Is Economically Efficient.* Economic strength does not come from power and firmness—but out of the cooperative flow of information within a corporate community.

*making the information is power* [handwritten]

*Implications for Healthcare by its old procurement system* [handwritten]

> *Principle 3: Progress Is Guided by Knowledge and Spirit.* Abundance is not the result of material riches—but of understanding the subtle workings of an infinitely complex world.

These are the new laws governing institutions today, the economic imperatives that determine who succeeds and who fails, the keys to pioneering an unexplored frontier of boundless knowledge—*The Infinite Resource.*

## The Coming Economic Passage

Grasping the enormity of these ideas will challenge corporate managers, government officials, scholars, and the rest of us for years. Many will not survive this test of history. But the relentless growth of IT should continue to drive change. Nicholas Negroponte, director of MIT's Media Lab, considers IT "a force of nature that cannot be stopped, the ultimate triumph of decentralization, globalization, and empowerment."[2]

Later I will sum up my forecasts suggesting that major advances in IT will enter the mainstream sometime during the next few years. At the conclusion of this book, we will examine how the forces unleashed by this onslaught of technology are likely to drive three revolutions corresponding with the logic of these three principles: revolutions from control to freedom, from conflict to community, and from materialism to spirit.

As these changes reach a critical mass of people and organizations, we are likely to witness a reversal in economic thought roughly during the years 2000–2005—it should be experienced as "passing through the eye of a needle."

## What Replaces the Hierarchy?

Scholars and executives pointed out for decades that an upheaval was imminent in organizations,[3] but the idea was not taken seriously until about 1990 when IT erupted into a revolutionary force, spreading electronic markets and relentless competition around the globe. Now, new corporate practices are emerging almost daily, government is being "reinvented," educational bureaucracies are struggling to change, and health care has entered a state of upheaval.

These events have shattered the comfortable old way we once viewed the world, driving home the realization that societies are facing fundamental change. The Information Revolution is transforming our entire social order, just as the Industrial Revolution transformed the feudal order two centuries ago. The significance of this onslaught of history cannot be overstated. A new age in management, institutions, and society is at hand.[4]

It's rather obvious now that the hierarchical organization that dominated history is passing rapidly, if not already dead. The collapse of communism is but the most visible failure of hierarchy everywhere, including the decline of former corporate bureaucracies and the anti-big-government sentiment in almost all nations.

But management today is adrift as it struggles through conflicting ideas and difficult issues—even as the level of turbulence, diversity, and change is poised to explode when the Knowledge Revolution reaches full force in a few years.

## Management Is Swamped in Confusion

Although we have learned to improve quality, reengineer processes, form teams, and build networks of alliances, people are often swamped in confusion over today's constantly shifting maze of diverse management concepts—the "flavor of the month" syndrome.

It is estimated that thirty-one thousand gurus are advising companies on wildly different approaches to management, including "The Wisdom of Wolves," "Leadership Secrets of Attila the Hun," and even Indian tribal ceremonies. The flood of new management ideas is so great that scholars find no agreement on a coherent management paradigm, and some are hard at work forming a "theory of fads."[5]

The problem becomes apparent when one tries to pin down in sound business terms the operating principles for popular ideas such as organizational networks. Who holds the authority for major decisions in such systems? How will we know if the "nodes" in a network create value or destroy it? How is performance evaluated? Accountability ensured? Rewards and resources allocated? And so on.

If the answer is that top management handles these issues, what is really different? Isn't this merely a more flexible version of the hierarchy with most of the same disadvantages? After all, the old Industrial Age hulks of GM and IBM were awash in powerful alliances with clever partners even as they floundered in bureaucracy. If the answer is that people are free to do what they think best, what prevents anarchy? Achieving consensus among thousands of employees? Sheer good will?

Despite all the brave talk of "empowering" people to "network" in "learning organizations," the fact is that most companies remain largely controlled from the top—even though we now understand that the bulk of knowledge exists at lower ranks. It is refreshing to see other prominent scholars finally acknowledge this problem. Years ago I wrote, "The chief executive is usually the chief bottleneck." In 1996, Gary Hamel wrote in the *Harvard Business Review*, "The bottleneck is at the top."[6]

## Lack of Solutions to Chronic Problems

These conflicts are also responsible for our lack of good answers to chronic problems caused by today's restructuring, which has become notorious for entrenched resistance, meager economic gains, over-burdened staffs, badly served clients, and alienated people. Restructuring is certainly needed, but present approaches focus on layoffs and cost cutting imposed on workers who have little to gain from these measures—at the very time that managers also know they must empower people, encourage collaboration, and cultivate knowledge.

A similar contradiction is destroying the legitimacy of corporate leaders. Though executive pay has reached celebrity levels, employee pay has been flat for two decades and one-third of the work force is struggling with marginal, low-paid jobs. When Robert Allen fired forty thousand workers while pocketing $3 million, AT&T suffered such damage to its reputation that the company plunged to the bottom of *Fortune*'s annual ranking of Most Admired Companies. *Business Week* noted, "Making 200 times the average paycheck . . . doesn't generate respect."[7]

The prevailing criticism is nicely seen in the comic strip Dilbert. Cartoonist Scott Adams turned the absurdities of today's management into a humorous form of protest, making the strip a national icon representing smart young employees struggling against confused, self-serving managers. Adams may exaggerate a bit, but Dilbert captures the public's low opinion of management today.

## The Big Changes Are Yet to Come

Most importantly, prevailing concepts are not likely to withstand the massive changes looming ahead.

The spreading of IT has unleashed hypercompetition to create a frontier of new products, markets, and services that nobody really understands as yet. Entire industries, such as banking, media, and education, are entering some poorly grasped and widely feared upheaval. Electronic education is making today's classrooms obsolete, for instance, and so across the land academics are baffled over how to redefine what they should do, where this is going, and what it means. The liberating power of information systems is also unleashing a reservoir of employee resentment to undermine old power structures. One CEO held an electronic meeting over the company's intranet only to see executives attacked so viciously that he had to pull the plug.[8]

Can organizations cope with this tidal wave of revolutionary change without motivated workers and inspiring leadership? How will we understand what's needed without seeing the full scope of this historic transition? One of the biggest obstacles is that managers do not generally understand how to create a different breed of bottom-up entrepreneurial organizations, and they have a hard time believing that people would behave responsibly without direct control. The result is that today's interest in management innovation is often little more than fashion and good intentions. The gap between rhetoric and reality is vast. To make matters worse, this entire topic is taboo for discussion because it involves the sensitive issue of power, adding to the abundant confusion that thrives in management today.

This dilemma will resist solution as long as we continue to think about management within a hierarchical, profit-centered framework. Major corporations comprise economic systems that are as large and complex as national economies, yet they are commonly controlled from the top down: defining strategic initiatives, moving resources and people around, setting financial targets, and monitoring department budgets. How does this differ from the central planning that failed under communism? Why would such control be bad for a national economy but good for a corporate economy? Can *any* fixed structure be useful in a world of constant change?

The question cannot be avoided: How are we going to manage this infinite power of revolutionary knowledge if we don't know what replaces the hierarchy?

## Free and Infinite

In 1997, as this book goes to press, I think we are roughly halfway through this transition, but the most wrenching adjustments still lie ahead. As we will see, IT is gathering force for its final assault on our crumbling institutional foundations, which should then clear the way for the construction of dramatically different organizations at about the end of this decade. With hard work we will soon be there: a world in which most people focus their talents and energies on nothing less than managing data, information, knowledge, strategy, and vision.

A great deal has been said about the Information Revolution, globalization, and economic restructuring, so what is really new? Modern societies have been using powerful information technologies such as radio, telephone, and TV for many decades, global trade has been growing faster than national economies since World War II, and corporations are always changing. What is there about today's innovations that seems so unusually powerful and historic?

Previous economic revolutions exploited a new technology to improve life, but there were severe limits. The Agrarian Revolution spawned civilization by providing secure food supplies—but people still lived in primitive conditions and fought over limited resources. The Industrial Revolution harnessed machines to provide material goods—at the cost of even more severe problems such as the threats of nuclear war and environmental destruction.

The Information Revolution is fundamentally different because it taps a resource that is almost limitless and especially powerful. Unlike physical resources—land, labor, and capital—knowledge is constantly being created and the supply is inexhaustible, so it resolves the age-old clash over limited means. I think it is accurate to say that—for the first time—we have access to a vital resource that is boundless.

The potential is so great because IT offers a more powerful way of understanding an infinitely complex world. Science is revealing an unfathomable depth of intricate life throughout the universe, from the microscopic domain of minute organisms to the outer reaches of space and to the inner world of human consciousness. As physicist Freeman Dyson put it, the complexity of life stretches "Infinite in All Directions."⁹

Beyond sheer understanding, scientific knowledge permits controlling information systems that guide the behavior of living creatures and social systems—the very stuff that organizes life. Consider our growing ability to modify the genetic code that choreographs the growth and placement of trillions of constantly changing cells forming any organism, from insect to human. We can increasingly influence the human mind itself—the most complex object in the known universe—by seeing it as a beautifully packaged, chemical-electronic-optical computer operating a dense network of circuits and databases. Even civilization evolves around the accumulated knowledge embodied in technology—the printing press, the internal combustion engine, and the computer—guided by still more information systems such as democratic government and the modern corporation.

If all this information has been used for such common purposes over millennia, what is special today? The Information Revolution is our first serious attempt to make knowledge the main task of entire societies. Yes, the earliest writings of humans on stone tablets were a form of IT, but never have we used so many machines of such great power. The world in 1997 employed almost one billion PCs, each more powerful than the mainframes that formerly occupied entire rooms, cost millions of dollars, and required teams to operate. And the really big changes are yet to come. Andy Grove, CEO of Intel, claims that "computer power will soon be practically free and practically infinite."[10]

Thus, the unique thing about this transition is that we are witnessing today the slow but steady flowering of a remarkably different world of boundless potential. The possibilities for increasing human capabilities, prosperity, and social progress are so vast that most people find them unimaginable, too good to be true. Lawrence Kudlow, former budget official of the U.S. government and now a chief corporate economist, says, "Everyone is too pessimistic." Bill Gates told one hundred American CEOs at a private meeting that IT will "fulfill their wildest dreams."[11]

But what about the inevitable counterforces of risk and chaos? Because such power is almost certain to exceed our boldest estimates, we are likely to be surprised by an impending tidal wave of change that will dazzle our imaginations and test our abilities. Little wonder that we are having trouble figuring out what to do.


## The Principles of Enterprise, Cooperation, and Knowledge

This book draws on the views of leading executives, academics, and consultants to mark a clearer path through today's economic jungle. Most of the chapters were presented at a conference, "Creating the New Organization," held at the George Washington University campus in Washington, D.C., and attended by two hundred managers from the private and public sectors.

The meeting incorporated elements of a "virtual conference" by beaming in "electronic dialogues" with prominent business leaders such as Peter Drucker. Our intent was to create a vivid sense of the information-rich environment we will all use increasingly.

The book is not a summary of the proceedings but a collection of the best available thought on this important subject. Starting with the original talks, we obtained additional speeches, publications, and interviews from our speakers to make each chapter as fresh and complete as possible. Other authorities who did not attend the conference were invited to contribute in order to round out our coverage. In addition to this book, a CD-ROM was produced to provide the rich learning experience of interactive multimedia. Our hope is that the resulting book/CD-ROM package will offer a definitive source of information on this crucial topic.

But what is special about this book? What does it give readers that differs from the more than one hundred thousand others offered on the altar of the literary market each year?

In this introductory chapter, I present the principles of progress now emerging to define the "New Management" needed for an Information Age, or what scholars call a "theory of the firm" for a knowledge-based economy.[12]

The bulk of the book then offers the experiences, ideas, and suggestions of the leaders I've assembled to represent a cross section of progressive thought. As the table of contents shows, this discussion is organized into three parts that each focus more fully on one of the principles outlined in this chapter.

Part I shows that today's hierarchical structures are being replaced by an emerging foundation of management based on *enterprise*. The complexity of a knowledge era has made our old command-and-control systems obsolete, and so entrepreneurial freedom is now crucial, not only in economic systems but also to permit free enterprise in organizational systems.

Part II illustrates how entrepreneurial organizations must also use *cooperation* to form collaborative communities. Knowledge differs from physical resources because it increases when shared, making collaborative working relations productive not only in strategic alliances but between buyer and seller, employee and employer, business and government, and other stakeholders.

Part III describes the intelligent infrastructures now being built to guide this corporate community in creating powerful forms of *knowledge*. As we use knowledge more widely, it is also becoming clear that modern economies are entering a more abstract realm of understanding that can only be navigated by a sense of purpose, values, and other manifestations of the human spirit.

## Part I: Creating the Internal Enterprise System

One of the least understood aspects of the New Management is the way autonomous business units, cross-functional teams, intrapreneurship, internal customers, and other entrepreneurial features are being used to energize organizations. If we intend to avoid the top-down disadvantages of hierarchy, a fundamentally different type of organization is needed based on principles of *enterprise*. This concept is profound because it logically leads to forming complete "internal market economies."

Many progressive firms have developed various versions of this basic idea, as illustrated by the chapters of Steve Goldsmith, Russell Ackoff, and the Pinchots; the cases of Alcoa, Lufthansa, Koch, SAIC; and the other examples I've explored more fully elsewhere.[13] Rather than think in hierarchical terms—of departments, divisions, and the like—units are defined as "internal enterprises" or what the Pinchots call "intraprises." Like all enterprises, the key to success is clearly agreed-upon standards of accountability, the widest possible entrepreneurial freedom, and the support of corporate systems and leaders. Forced by the necessity to cope with a complex new era, a variety of leading organizations have moved toward this concept, as shown in Box I.1.

Rather than a fixed structure, this is an *economic process* or *self-organizing metastructure* that constantly evolves to offer all the

## BOX I.1.  EXEMPLARS OF INTERNAL ENTERPRISE

### Dynamic Corporations

A long list of dynamic corporations has adopted various aspects of internal enterprise, including MCI, Xerox, Johnson & Johnson, Hewlett-Packard, Motorola, Alcoa, and Clark Equipment. Recently, General Motors withstood a labor strike to give its auto divisions the power of internal customers able to choose outside suppliers over GM units.

### Internal Labor Markets

Intel, 3Com, and Raychem post job openings to allow the best person to find each position. Workers are organized into self-managed teams that are paid for their performance and free to choose their leaders, coworkers, methods, and all other aspects of their work.

### Outsourcing and Insourcing

A powerful trend toward enterprise is outsourcing to external suppliers and insourcing to internal enterprises. Volkswagen's new "world beater" plant in Rio de Janeiro has 80 percent of its production work done by employees of VW suppliers—outsourcing within companies.

### Entrepreneurial Government

Governments around the world are being transformed into entrepreneurial systems. In the United States, agencies such as the Department of Defense, General Services Administration, and Government Printing Office are privatizing formerly monopolistic functions to encourage a healthy dose of internal competition.

### School Choice

Schools are on the verge of an entrepreneurial revolution as parental choice, voucher systems, and charter schools replace the old bureaucracies with principles of enterprise.

### Abroad

Japanese firms are doing business outside of their keiretsu families and moving to merit pay. Matsushita turned its research labs, product groups, and sales offices into self-supporting units that do business with one another. Siemens and Lufthansa are among German firms that have adopted the internal market concept recently, and Semco has done the same in Brazil.

*Source:* William E. Halal and others, *Internal Markets* (New York: Wiley, 1993).

advantages of markets: accountability for results, entrepreneurial freedom, incentives for achievement, rapid response time, customer focus, creativity, and the like. Charles Handy calls it a "contractual organization."[14] Because of its flexibility, the internal market concept provides an economic foundation that also facilitates other innovative practices, such as networks, alliances, and virtual relationships.

It is important to note that there are no perfect organizational designs; internal markets incur the same disorder, risk, and general turmoil as external markets. The idea is not useful in military operations, space launches, and other situations requiring close coordination of thousands of people and intricate plans, nor in routine operations facing a relatively simple, stable environment. Thus, organizations will have to trade off the costs and gains of hierarchy versus enterprise. The prudent executive will combine varying degrees of control and freedom to find the mix that best suits the organization.

The chapters in Part I offer a variety of case studies to help us grasp this dramatically different perspective:

*Stephen Goldsmith*, Mayor of Indianapolis and arguably the most creative politician in America, describes how he transformed the city bureaucracy into a dynamic network of internal enterprises that compete with external suppliers of public services.

*Russell Ackoff*, chairman of INTERACT and one of the deans of modern management, defines the market perspective and offers examples of how it is being used in progressive firms.

*John Starr*, former president of an Alcoa division, tells us how he vitalized his insulated company by creating an enterprise system in which all internal suppliers and customers were set free to buy from and sell to external competitors.

*Wayne Gable*, manager of government affairs at Koch Enterprises, one of the world's largest private companies, describes the principles of market-based management that this firm has practiced for years.

*Mark Lehrer*, Research Fellow, Social Science Center Berlin, presents a case relating how Lufthansa used market mechanisms to rejuvenate its flagging operations.

## Part II: Forming a Network of Cooperative Alliances

Part II extends our understanding of strategic alliances with suppliers and business partners to include collaborative relations with employees, customers, and government. James Moore put it this way: "Competition as we've known it is dead."[15] Gerald Taylor at MCI, Ray Miles, Jessica Lipnack and Jeffery Stamps, Terri Holbrooke of Novell, Ron Oklewizc at Telepad, Bill Owens at SAIC, and the Pinchots explore this theme in their chapters. I then argue that the logical conclusion is tightly knit "corporate communities" that join the interests of all stakeholders into productive coalitions.

But what about the traditional "tough" approach to business? Why would centuries of economic conflict change? Because the Information Revolution is overthrowing this old system as surely as the Industrial Revolution overthrew the medieval economic system.

Just as the assembly line shifted the critical factor of production from labor to capital, the computer is shifting the critical factor of production from capital to knowledge. Knowledge differs because the marginal cost of duplicating it is trivial and its value *increases*

## BOX I.2. EXEMPLARS OF CORPORATE COOPERATION
### Research Consortia

About 250 research consortia and 1,600 business-government research agreements have been formed in the United States. The auto industry alone has twelve consortia in which all three major car makers work together on developing everything from new fuels to electric cars.

### Supplier and Distributor Alliances

Companies such as Nike, Dell, Chrysler, Caterpillar, and Novell have improved operations by forming close relationships with suppliers and distributors.

### Employee Collaboration

Raychem, Intel, Motorola, and other firms consider collaborative employee relations a key corporate strategy. They provide training, employee freedom, and attractive rewards to reduce costs, improve sales, and generate knowledge.

### Relationship Marketing

Progressive firms form a trusting relationship with clients that focuses on delivering value and engaging customers in the company. A good example is the picnic Saturn held for thirty thousand Saturn owners.

### Partnerships with Competitors

While GM, Ford, and Chrysler compete against Toyota, Renault, and Fiat, they also jointly design, make, and sell cars with these same adversaries. A similar blend of cooperation and competition marks relations between IBM and Apple, Nucor and USX, TI and Hitachi.

### Economic Coalitions and Ecosystems

Companies such as Microsoft and Netscape organize economic coalitions uniting suppliers, manufacturers, distributors, and others in a cluster of cooperating firms centered around a major product.

### Business-Government Partnerships

American cities such as Baltimore, San Antonio, and Indianapolis are forming partnerships with business, labor, and civic groups.

### Corporate Community

Some companies have united all these alliances into complete "corporate communities." GM Saturn, The Body Shop, and IKEA develop trusting relationships with clients, share power with workers, cooperate with suppliers and dealers, and form partnerships with government while also making superior profits for their investors.

*Source:* William E. Halal, *The New Management* (San Francisco: Berrett-Koehler, 1996).

when shared, making cooperation advantageous to all parties. This new economic reality is leading to the realization that cooperation is now *efficient* because it creates value. As the examples in Box I.2 illustrate, various collaborative alliances are thriving because they offer a competitive advantage.

The Information Age may reward cooperation, but the downside is that any union restricts autonomy, and so it may be unwise to form permanent ties. As the concluding chapter shows more fully, dynamic companies form alliances with alternative partners. They need the benefits of cooperation, yet they also want to avoid becoming dependent by maintaining the option of switching to others. So the principle of cooperation must be tempered by the equally important principle of dynamic enterprise.

The chapters in Part II highlight different facets of this blend of enterprise and collaborative alliances:

> *Gerald Taylor,* CEO of MCI, describes how high-tech companies must focus on creating and distributing knowledge through collaborative alliances, roughly the way Industrial Age companies were organized to create and distribute goods.

> *Ray Miles,* former dean of the Berkeley Business School, reports on his continuing studies of network organizations, recently identifying an exciting new form of "spherical" structure.

> *Jessica Lipnack and Jeffrey Stamps,* coauthors of *The Age of the Network,* present their latest thoughts on the principles of effective network management.

> *Terri Holbrooke,* former senior vice president for marketing at Novell, shares her experience managing the alliance between Novell and WordPerfect and notes the special power of sharing knowledge.

*Ron Oklewizc*, CEO of Telepad, Inc., describes the struggles required to manage a wide range of difficult partnerships involved in a virtual corporation.

## Part Three: Leveraging Knowledge with an Intelligent Infrastructure

The importance of knowledge is highlighted by the fact that the value of various knowledge assets rose from 38 percent of corporate assets in 1982 to 62 percent in 1992. Human capital alone, the value-producing power of employee know-how, is estimated to account for 70 percent of all wealth in modern economies. Adding in intellectual property (patents and the like), brand names, and other forms of knowledge brings the total to more than 80 percent of corporate assets. The problem is that managers think only about 20 percent of this strategic asset is used.[16]

To be more effective, an "intelligent infrastructure" is needed to support the entrepreneurial community just described in Parts One and Two above. But this requires more than the organizational learning of individuals or teams; it is the learning of an entire corporate *system* to produce "organizational intelligence" (OI), a higher equivalent of human intelligence.

How can we increase an entire organization's ability to learn? By using IT to unite collaborative enterprises into a total learning system. It is now possible to combine high-performing information networks and dynamic organization structures to produce an unusual capacity to amass raw information from diverse sources, store it in common databases, distill the data into valuable knowledge, and allow units to retrieve it from any part of the network. The principles of enterprise and cooperation would provide the management system, and a distributed network of PCs operating on an intranet would provide the information system. The chapters by Ray Smith at Bell Atlantic, David Walters from Oklahoma, Michael Malone, Bob Kuperman at Chiat/Day, and Bill Owens at SAIC offer good illustrations of intelligent infrastructures.

Please note that an intelligent infrastructure must include more than powerful information systems. Equally indispensable is the human half of the organization noted in Parts I and II—all those entrepreneurial and cooperative activities that take place when small groups of people meet to solve problems, trade ideas, and help one another. These messy human interactions make up "tacit" knowledge as opposed to the well-structured "explicit" or "formal" knowledge stored in information systems. Tacit knowledge is indispensable because this is the way people actually think, whether it is employees doing their work, customers making purchases, or managers solving organizational problems.[17]

Xerox's famed Palo Alto Research Center (PARC) laboratory discovered that small "communities of practice" (CPs) form the basic unit of innovation. CPs are close-knit groups of like-minded people who manage themselves as a small enterprise devoted to perfecting some set of skills. This highlights how the close relationships that mark employee work teams, a group of engineers or scientists, a sales force, or a board of directors are crucial to the creative learning that takes place in any organizational unit. Similar relationships *across* units and entire organizations are also essential to move knowledge from one CP to another, as when firms work with their customers, suppliers and distributors, and other stakeholders. Jack Welch described this as the goal of GE's famous boundaryless organization: "The only way to be more competitive is to engage every mind in the organization."[18]

A good intelligent infrastructure, therefore, consists of a corporate-wide information system and a web of close working relationships connecting entrepreneurial units to common pools of shared knowledge. The result is a "central nervous system" that leverages ordinary learning to powerful new levels, forming an intelligent organization. If we carry this line of thought further, each individual becomes a node in this network, which then forms a "corporate brain" possessing powers of mass intelligence. Box I.3 offers some examples.

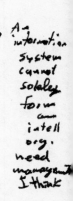

*An information system cannot solely form an intell org. need management I think*

The chapters in Part III draw on the pioneering innovations of executives from some of our most famous knowledge corporations to sketch out the features of intelligent infrastructures:

*Raymond Smith*, CEO and chairman of Bell Atlantic, outlines the new capabilities that are rolling off the Information Super-highway to revolutionize organizations and society.

*David Walters*, former governor of Oklahoma, tells us about the innovative government he created by using information technology to vastly improve the state's operations without increasing taxes.

*Michael Malone*, coauthor of *The Virtual Corporation*, shows how his landmark concept of virtual organizations is producing a revolutionary new form of business and economics.

*Elizabeth and Gifford Pinchot*, coauthors of *The Intelligent Organization*, offer their latest thinking on how to create organizational systems that think and act with greater power.

*Robert Kuperman*, CEO of Chiat/Day, relates his experience in forming one of the first virtual organizations and offers suggestions for other managers.

*William Owens*, president and COO of Science Applications International Corporation (SAIC), outlines the features that make this organization a model of what is to come soon.

## BOX I.3. EXEMPLARS OF KNOWLEDGE SYSTEMS
### McGraw-Hill's Information Turbine

McGraw-Hill created a corporate-wide information network, performance incentives, and training programs to unify all units into an "intellectual community," like a university or research lab. The central element was a knowledge base that pooled the information gathered by units, which they could then draw on to serve their clients better—aptly called an "information turbine" because it converted raw data into a stream of knowledge that "powered" the organization.

### Hewlett-Packard's Knowledge Systems

HP has developed a Computer Systems Marketing Organization to share product information, market data, and strategic ideas. A Corporate Information Systems unit is putting all management procedures and personnel practices onto a World Wide Web site and Lotus Notes. A system called Knowledge Links supports product divisions with purchasing services, engineering data, market intelligence, and best practices. All this is unified by a "World Innovation Network" that allows employees to probe each other's experiences on what works.

### Merrill Lynch's Database

The world's largest security broker helps its eighteen thousand account managers operating in five hundred offices serve their millions of clients with a computer network that stores the firm's knowledge base about securities, financial forecasts, and the like.

### IBM's IS Services

IBM's CIO uses a corporate intranet to provide units with evaluations of suppliers and to match corporate buyers with sellers. All IBM purchasing is being conducted over the net, saving $1 billion per year.

### Andersen Consulting's Practice Pool

Andersen uses a global network called Knowledge Xchange to pool the experiences and best practices of its worldwide consulting practice. The CIO said, "Our clients should get the best knowledge in the firm, not just the best in their consultant."

*Sources:* Thomas Davenport, "Some Principles of Knowledge Management," *Strategy & Business* (Winter 1996), pp. 34–41; James Quinn and others, "Managing Professional Intellect," *Harvard Business Review* (Mar.–Apr. 1996), pp. 71–83; "Jack Welch's Cyber-Czar," *Business Week* (Aug. 5, 1996), pp. 82–83.

## On the Other Side

Throughout these chapters, the emphasis is on promising new concepts, lessons gained from experience, and suggestions on moving forward. But most importantly, my coauthors and I have grappled with the difficult issues presented by this historic transition. Please join me at the end of this book when my concluding chapter attempts to make sense out of all these diverse ideas.

We will see that life should be different on the other side of this passage. When the dust settles in a decade or so, business, government, and other institutions are likely to become decentralized clusters of internal enterprise units operating from the bottom up to self-manage complexity, thereby driving innovation continuously throughout society. They will also be integrated symbiotically with their various stakeholders, forming tight-knit but shifting communities of diverse economic actors. And the entire system will focus sharply on leveraging knowledge to guide strategies that serve social as well as financial goals.

It may help to think of this as a somewhat refined amalgam of three prominent corporations that represents a new theory of the firm able to master the difficult times ahead—the dynamic enterprise of MCI, combined with the collaborative working relations of Saturn, all guided by the intelligence of Microsoft.

Speaking personally, I can think of no more worthwhile goal, and so I feel enormously pleased to present the thoughts of such a distinguished array of associates to address such crucial issues at such a fascinating time in history. I hope you will find the chapters that follow equally worthwhile.

## Notes

1. William E. Halal and others, *Internal Markets: Bringing the Power of Free Enterprise Inside Your Organization* (New York: Wiley, 1993).

2. Nicholas Negroponte, *Being Digital* (New York: Knopf, 1995).

3. For instance, Peter Drucker, *The Age of Discontinuity* (New York: Harper & Row, 1968); Warren Bennis, *Beyond Bureaucracy* (New York: McGraw-Hill, 1966); Daniel Bell, *The Coming of Post-Industrial Society* (New York: Basic Books, 1973); and Alvin Toffler, *The Third Wave* (New York: Bantam Books, 1980).

4. William E. Halal, *The New Capitalism* (New York: Wiley, 1986).

5. John Micklewait and Adrian Woolridge, *The Witch Doctors: Making Sense of the Management Gurus* (New York: Times Books, 1996); Jeffrey Pfeffer, "Barriers to the Advance of Organizational Science," *Academy of Management Review* (Oct. 1993) Vol. 18, No. 4, pp. 599–621.

6. My comment appeared in William E. Halal, *The New Capitalism* (New York: Wiley, 1986), p. 128. Hamel is quoted from Gary Hamel, "Strategy as Revolution," *Harvard Business Review* (July–Aug. 1996), pp. 69–82.

7. "Executive Pay," *Business Week* (Apr. 21, 1997).

8. Amy E. Schwartz, "Learning Civility in Cyberspace," *Washington Post* (Dec. 16, 1994); Michael Schrage, "How to Take the Organizational Temperature," *Wall Street Journal* (Nov. 7, 1994).

9. Freeman Dyson, *Infinite in All Directions* (New York: Harper & Row, 1989).

10. Grove is quoted from "A Conversation with the Lords of Wintel," *Fortune* (July 8, 1996).

11. *New York Times* (May 10, 1997).

12. William E. Halal, *The New Management* (San Francisco: Berrett-Koehler, 1996).

13. William E. Halal and others, *Internal Markets: Bringing the Power of Free Enterprise Inside Your Organization* (New York: Wiley, 1993).

14. Charles Handy, *Understanding Organizations* (New York: Oxford University Press, 1993).

15. James Moore, *The Death of Competition* (New York: HarperCollins, 1996).

16. Thomas Stewart, "Trying to Grasp the Intangible," *Fortune* (Oct. 2, 1996), pp. 157–161; Polly LaBarre, "The Rush to Knowledge," *Industry Week* (Feb. 19, 1996).

17. Hirotake Takeuchi and Ikujiro Nonaka, *The Knowledge-Creating Company* (New York: Oxford University Press, 1995).

18. Thomas Stewart, "The Invisible Key to Success," *Fortune* (Aug. 5, 1996), pp. 173–176.

# Part I

# Creating the Internal Enterprise System

# 1

# A Small Government Solution
# to Big City Problems

## Stephen Goldsmith

Cities need to change for some pretty simple reasons. First, they are no longer competitive with their suburbs. Cities used to compete with each other, but now they compete with other areas in their own region. As a result, large inner-city areas are suffering severe population declines. It is not very difficult for people to pack up their home or business and move across city boundaries. In most large midwestern cities, such as St. Louis, Cleveland, and Detroit, we have seen population declines of 30 to 40 percent over the past ten years.

Inner cities are also facing a great loss of capital. In 1980, per capita income in cities was 90 percent of what it was in nearby suburbs. In 1990 that figure was down to 59 percent.

Since becoming mayor of Indianapolis in 1992, Stephen Goldsmith has created the best working model of city governance in America. Focusing on the introduction of modern management methods, public-private sector competition, and effective performance evaluation, the number of city employees was reduced by 26 percent while services to citizens were improved. The city's budget decreased even as the population grew, permitting substantial new investment in adding more police, rebuilding infrastructure, and improving poor neighborhoods. Because the city now functions so well, forty major companies relocated to Indianapolis and unemployment is down.

Although most suburban governments and their citizens are not very receptive to metropolitan-wide solutions, the fact is that the well-being of suburbs is closely tied to their inner cities. Studies have shown that suburbs may benefit in the short term by taking city jobs and people, but in a decade or so the prosperity of the entire region will fall if it does not possess a vital urban core.

This erosion of population and wealth in our major cities will continue if we manage them the way we did before. They will fail, possibly at even faster rates. Most politicians today promise not to raise taxes or offer some version of this basic idea. I suggest that for city governments this is more than a wishful hope, it is an economic imperative. Studies of cities such as Philadelphia show that if you raise property taxes, over time government income will decline. People with money move, which increases the tax burden on those remaining and lowers their incomes, which then sends the appraised value of business and homes down. This in effect sends the tax rate up, encouraging even more people to move and thereby perpetuating a downward spiral.

The basic problem, then, is how to create wealth in our cities.

## There Is No Substitute for Competition

One of the best ways is to become more client oriented and to dramatically cut the cost of living and doing business in a city. That is essentially what we have done in Indianapolis.

Just as competition is urging business to show that it is more customer-oriented, people are demanding more responsive performance on the part of governments. As we search for more effective ways to organize life in an Information Age, one of the first things we should do is to break up large, unresponsive, monopolistic governments.

About 220 mayors, governors, and representatives of foreign countries have visited Indianapolis to observe what we are doing, and I've also had many invitations to visit them. I was on my way to see Mayor Giuliani of New York recently. As you drive into Manhattan from LaGuardia Airport, at the first set of stoplights, pan-handlers purporting to be car windshield washers approach with great aggressiveness. The taxi driver was clearly experienced at handling this situation, and he did not like it. When the light changed and this man reached in the car to collect his "fee," the taxi driver muttered some harsh words as he gave the man a bit of change and drove away rapidly.

It struck me that this is roughly what government has become today. We furnish services that the public does not always want, and then we force people to pay for these services even if they are unneeded and badly delivered. We need to return government to its essence by providing a smaller range of more customer-oriented services that truly serve human needs.

I have received much recognition for the way we've managed the Indianapolis city government, but it has not really been that difficult. We just study how corporations have learned to manage themselves better, and then we do the same. Over the past few years, we have learned TQM methods, delayered our old hierarchy, created teams, and applied the rest of today's management innovations. But I have learned that nothing improves government more than the introduction of competition.

The problem is not that those in private enterprise are inherently better than those of us in public life. It is that the private sector operates in a more competitive environment. Monopoly in government creates the high overhead rates and the lack of responsiveness people complain of, not the difference between public employees and private employees. What we need to do is break up those monopolies and compete on the basis of services provided. The competition may be among internal or external service providers in city government, or between city and state governments, or private versus public enterprise. If we can do that, we will help public employees learn how to be more productive.

When I was elected, we invited nine of Indianapolis's most entrepreneurial business men and women to be part of a commission. We also gave them volunteer MBAs, JDs, and CPAs to help and asked them to audit our city government, identify each distinctive business function, estimate how much it costs us to run each business, and tell us which ones could be outsourced. We found that we manage about two hundred different business services in Indianapolis. We examined all units, looked at their performance, and competed out some services. Competition dramatically reduced our overhead rates.

For example, we have a street maintenance division. Motorists often reported seeing three supervisors watching three workers fill a pothole along the side of a road. So we decided to open up that function to competition. The union local president said, "If you are going to load the salaries of all those supervisors onto our costs when we bid, we can't compete. Right now, we have ninety-four truck drivers and thirty-two supervisors. We would like you to remove eighteen supervisors."

Now, this was a difficult political situation that posed a critical test of my philosophy because those supervisors had supported me while the union had opposed me. Nevertheless, we went forward and laid off the eighteen supervisors. Then a group of workers came in and said, "By the way, we have eight people working on two trucks, but we really could do the same amount of work if we had five people on one truck." We said okay.

This unit then submitted a proposal based on the revised number of supervisors and workers, and they won the competition decisively. It turned out that they outperformed their private-sector competitors for that street resurfacing project because their costs came down 25 percent from what they were before we opened the job to competition. And this was after six years of rigorous TQM practice, during which none of these suggestions came up for discussion.

Contrary to conventional beliefs, this did not alienate our local union because its members were eager to apply their talents to doing a better job, and they were rewarded. Pay and benefits for city employees have gone up, and the executive director of our union has become a partner in this effort.

*← A main theme*

To reinforce the importance of competition over monopoly, let me give you another short example. Before I was elected, we had both public and private city garbage workers organized into eight franchised monopolies. The city negotiated with each of the providers. We believed that it is good to have a mix of public and private employees. Then we decided to compete out the franchises among this same group of providers. The cost per household came down by 20 percent, or $15 million, over the length of the contract. In fact, the public trash haulers actually expanded their routes as a result of the competitive process, and their employees have received bonuses averaging $1,750.

Now, this is not to say that the city workers got all the contracts, but it is to say that a monopoly—either public or private—does not produce maximum value. We have tried to move our government in the direction of competition. This is the same direction that schools are moving in through choice and charter schools, as well as other areas of government. So we know that competition has to become a central tenet of good public service.

We also know that this process of competition can apply technology to create value. Let me offer another example. We have two large wastewater plants in my city. They are today the largest, most sophisticated plants in the country, primarily because we are the largest city that is not located on a real river. We have something that we call a river, the White River, but it is much smaller, and so we have to treat the water. It happens that my city council does not share my enthusiasm for these competition initiatives. They wanted to hire a Big Six accounting firm and let it evaluate how efficient we are. So we did. The firm reviewed our plant operations and concluded that we were among the most efficient wastewater treatment plants in the country: "You could not improve the efficiency of these plants more than 5 to 10 percent no matter what you do," said the firm.

The study was nice but irrelevant because the question in my mind was, "What could the market offer on this particular service?" We obtained bids from five of the largest providers in the world. They were happy to compete because it turns out that ours was the

largest wastewater plant in the world. So we accepted the best proposal to manage the plant, and the cost of our water treatment operations came down 44 percent, or $65 million over five years, making
ours one of the most efficient public water treatment systems anywhere. The number of employees has fallen by half, but they have
higher pay and benefits, safety is far better, and there are virtually
no union complaints.

Why? Because the level of technology available in the worldwide market is so much better than that available locally for the
usual applications of a small city government. The winner of the
competition was a partnership that included a large French water
treatment company that uses much more sophisticated technology,
thereby producing huge savings. Had we not searched widely for
competitors, we would never have reached this level of sophistication. So the process of competition can draw on world markets to
bring the highest level of technology into play for local applications.

## The Need for Economic Information

Government innovation also can be introduced in other ways.
Competition presumes that we know what our costs are. You cannot compete if you do not know what your costs are. When I was
elected, we had the best-looking certified financial reports of any
city. The color separators and the quality of the paper were unpar-
alleled, and the numbers balanced at the bottom of each page. We
had a triple-A credit rating. But there was nothing in these reports
available to tell me how much it cost to clean a mile of sewer, to
take a picture using microfilm, or to print a brochure. There was
absolutely no useful costing data available.

So we hired an outside firm that rigorously went through our
government to create activity-based costing systems. Now we really
know what our costs are in government—not what we guess our
costs are, but what our true costs are based on data. Competition is
not a very satisfactory process without this type of data because all
you are doing is fooling yourself.

Let me illustrate how this type of information presents wonderful opportunities for organizational change. One manager wrote to me—a man in charge of safety training for the public works department—and said, "We have a videotape operation in our shop. I would like to close it down and sell it." Now, this never happens. People inside any organization rarely say, "I am the supervisor of a section. Will you please close it down?" So we gave him an award, and I went down to visit his shop. We also invited the press because we wanted to focus attention on employees who are thinking clearly about their jobs.

One of the press people asked this man, "What led you to do this?" He said, "When we started to do activity-based costing, the mayor said he was going to put the cost of my building's rent into my budget, and he was going to allocate the depreciated cost of my equipment into my budget, as well as the salaries of my employees. I can go out and buy a training tape much more cheaply than I can produce a training tape myself with this video unit. So I need to close it down and get these costs out of my system. Then I can be more competitive."

Here is an employee who managed this system for ten years and never saw the problem. He is a good person in a bad system who—when challenged with real cost data—understood the problem and solved it. Activity costing has had a dramatic effect.

We can also urge innovation by using better performance measurements. The absence of performance data either in the private sector or government creates great difficulties. If you do not know what your outcomes or outputs are, if you do not have measures of where you are, then it is very difficult to talk about effectiveness, innovation, or anything really.

I invited a company to work with us that you might have read about in the *Wall Street Journal*. It's called America Works. I have been trying to reform the welfare system in Indianapolis for seven years unsuccessfully. I asked America Works to come in because I met the fellow who runs it, and he said, "If you hire me, I promise you will only have to pay me when I am successful." This was intriguing. Nobody had ever presented me this kind of proposal before. During our meeting he said, "I will take a person off of welfare, I will find that person a job, I will train the person, I will help the person apply, and I will make sure the person gets to work. And if the person works for six months, then you pay me the amount that is equal to the half of what they would have earned had they been on welfare for that six months." I said, "Move into town. I will fund that program."

He came into town, set up, and called me about two months later with a problem. He said, "We have a long list of employers who want employees, and we have successfully approved every application that has come through our shop. In the area of Indianapolis where we are working, there are 20,000 people on AFDC (or welfare) so they are interested. But the problem is that in the sixty days we have been working here, we've only received forty referrals from the city agencies. That's because the federal welfare department's performance is not measured on the basis of how many people find jobs, but on how many errors they make when they distribute the money."

So we had a performance-based organization on our side depending on referrals from a federal operation in our city that does not have sound performance standards or incentives. This drove home to us that we were unable to meet any reasonable vision of government performance without common economic standards throughout the city. Unless we connect performance to innovation, we are spinning our wheels in many different ways.[1]

There are many other such examples of our efforts. We privatized the Indianapolis Naval Air Warfare Center by encouraging the Navy to sell it to Hughes Technical Services, which saved the federal government $1 billion and kept this vital research facility alive.[2] We converted our many other bureaucratic operations into profitable enterprises, reduced regulations, and helped citizens take better care of their neighborhoods.[3]

My point is that although we can innovate most forcefully through competition, we cannot compete effectively unless we have activity-based costing and sound performance measures. Competition also drives technology advancements, and if we connect that with performance, as we do in our outsourced contracts, we can effectively drive innovation inside the system.

## Moving Ahead

We hear many complaints about this process. One is that, by reinventing functions into entrepreneurial activities and competing out, we may be only renovating a process or function that is outdated in the first place. This activity may not be useful or may not have to be done the way it is. That is, doing more efficiently a government service that should not be done at all is not really the best use of public time.

For example, one of my engineers in the sewer water department became caught up in the enthusiasm for outsourcing to solve a long backlog of building permits. This engineer thought, "Now I understand it. I have seen the light. I am going to outsource. I am going to hire a group of private engineers. I am going to tell them to approve these permits. I am going to get these permits done as quickly as they can and make up for our backlog." So he took the existing system and outsourced it. Six months later we had to pay out $500,000, yet we had cut our delays only by 10 to 15 percent—little gain for a huge cost.

What we should have done was reengineer the whole system to begin with. We should have eliminated a number of departmental handoffs, created teams, and then competed out the improved system. This is a frequent and serious complaint.

We are often criticized for the wastefulness of our private contractors. My experience has been that this problem is a direct failure of government oversight. Government must be sure that a task is well engineered and has quality standards, price standards, and trained people to manage the contract. Those correctives would often stop the problem or prevent it from arising altogether.

Another frequent complaint from the public or from other mayors or governors is that you can't outsource a critical function because you will then lose control over it. My view is that I can *gain* control by outsourcing if I am clear about what the quality is, and if the contract is clear about what I can do in terms of financial penalties and how I can terminate the contract. The aim of negotiating a contract is to specify desirable performance measures, and if it does not work I can always terminate the contract or fine the company. In this way, I find that what I do lose control over is patronage and unneeded employees. Losing those problems is a great blessing.

It is often said that middle managers are the most difficult to convince about the need for change, and that the cause is always a communication problem. But I would have to say that communication is not the main problem. The managers understand the situation very well. The choices are clear: we can become a leaner and more efficient government, which requires replacing a few of us; or we can outsource, which also replaces a few of us. Neither of those choices looked attractive to the managers, so they resisted because they did not see change as being in their interest.

The problem came to a head one day when we suffered a major problem over snow removal. Mayors are voted out of office because snow stays on the roads. We had particularly horrible snow removal delays twice last year, so I went out to visit everybody involved in the operation. I said, "I want all the managers to stay outside and I want all the truck drivers to come inside the room." I asked what went wrong. I got about fifty ideas: the salt we bought was inferior, the plows did not work right, the routes were wrong, and so on. I went to the next room with the managers and asked them what went wrong. They said nothing went wrong. They said they executed the plan exactly as we had devised it and people went out and did it.

Here we had ten years of TQM training, we had units competing for their work, the union thinking that jobs are at stake—and yet the managers thought nothing was wrong.

Well, now we are trying to infuse some of these changes in our managers. The focus is on training, changing, and delayering management, a very difficult task but nevertheless critical for allowing innovation to percolate through the system.

I also think that government and business need to realign their relationship. The traditional approach is that business waits for a request for proposal from government. Then it focuses only on how much it can charge, not on how much value it creates for citizens. Business doesn't think about how it can apply reengineering, technology, or other innovations by taking the initiative to suggest creative ideas to government. So a valuable source of innovation would be available if business firms could rethink their governmental relationships in value-added terms rather than just profit making.

The point is that all of our existing institutions—business, government, education, and others—will need to change, and we can make these changes better by working together more effectively. It is an exciting time. A technological revolution, growing competition, and a global economy are creating unprecedented challenges but also unprecedented opportunities. Now we have to be willing to take the risk of moving through the obstacles to realize a new future.

## Notes

1. Stephen Goldsmith, "End the Welfare Delivery Monopoly," *Wall Street Journal* (Aug. 23, 1994).

2. Stephen Goldsmith, "Designing a Smooth Privatization," *Wall Street Journal* (June 3, 1996).

3. For a full and detailed account of the changes introduced by Mayor Goldsmith, see *The Indianapolis Experience: A Small Government Prescription for Big City Problems* (City of Indianapolis: 1996).

# Transforming Organizations into Market Economies

## Russell L. Ackoff

The state of management practice today is highlighted by the fact that there are more panaceas than problems. Downsizing, reengineering, TQM, benchmarking, outsourcing, scenario planning, and so on represent only a partial list of the panaceas in good currency at the moment. However, there is a growing literature about their failure. A well-known study by Arthur D. Little and another by Ernst and Young showed that about two-thirds of TQM efforts have been disappointing. Other studies show that most downsizing efforts eventually increase costs, and so on.

---

Russell L. Ackoff, the chairman of INTERACT, is professor emeritus at the University of Pennsylvania and one of the deans of modern management thought. He cofounded the first U.S. graduate program in operations research at the Case Institute of Technology and the Social Systems Sciences Program at the University of Pennsylvania. He is the former president of the Operations Research Society and the Society for General Systems Research. Ackoff has authored twenty books and hundreds of articles, and consulted with more than four hundred corporations and governments. His most recent book is *The Democratic Corporation* (New York: Oxford University Press, 1994).

## The Need to View Organizations as Systems

Panaceas fail because they are antisystemic. A system is a whole that cannot be divided into independent parts. Its essential (defining) properties derive from the interactions of its parts, not their actions taken separately. If an automobile were disassembled, for example, it would lose all its essential properties even if all its parts were kept in one place. A disassembled automobile is no longer an automobile because it cannot function as one.

All the panaceas deal with parts or aspects of a system taken separately. It turns out that when we improve the parts of a system taken separately, we very seldom improve the performance of the system as a whole. This can be rigorously proven in system science, but it is not necessary. An example will do.

Suppose we gather in one place one of every automobile available in the United States. Then we have a group of the best automotive engineers determine which car has the best motor, then the best transmission, then the best distributor, and so on until we know for each essential part of an automobile which is the best available. Then suppose we have these parts removed from their source and try to assemble them into an automobile that consists of only the best parts available. We don't even get an automobile, let alone the best one, because *the parts don't fit.*

What can we conclude? The performance of a system depends on how its parts interact, not on how they act separately. Yet today's panaceas focus on improving parts considered independently of the system of which they are part. This may improve the performance of the part, but seldom of the whole.

Another fundamental problem is the important distinction Peter Drucker made between doing things right and doing the right thing. It is much better to do the right thing wrong than the wrong thing right. The righter we do the wrong thing, the wronger it becomes. For example, we continue to put more and more money into outmoded approaches to education and health care and succeed only in making them worse. But if we do the right thing wrong we have the opportunity to learn from an acknowledged mistake and improve the next time around.

There are many other examples of doing the wrong thing right, of increasing the efficiency with which we pursue the wrong objectives. For instance, the automobile is clearly a dysfunctional solution to the urban transportation problem. A visit to most major cities—for example, Mexico City, Santiago, Caracas, or New York—reveals why. Mexico City recently suffered a traffic jam that tied up thousands of cars for hours, during which several people died because of the inability to get medical attention to them. Mexican children are frequently kept home from school because the air pollution makes it dangerous for them to walk outside. Trees on the beautiful Avenida de Reforma have died of the same pollution.

The automobile is gradually destroying the quality of urban life around the world. Automobiles are designed to carry 4 to 6 people but carry only 1.2 on the average. They are designed for speeds in excess of one hundred miles per hour but travel in cities at about seventeen miles per hour on average. Passengers are faced forward when it has been shown that their safety is maximized when they sit facing backward. But we keep improving automobiles as currently conceived, hence continue to do the wrong thing righter.

All panaceas are concerned with changes in the existing system—with reform. In contrast, I want to talk about a change in the very *nature* of the system—about transformation. There is a fundamental difference between reforming an existing system and transforming it. Reformation simply produces a modified version of the existing system. Transformation produces a system different in form and function. Panaceas reform, never transform, an organization.

## A Systemic View of Corporate Economies

A number of problems facing enterprises cannot be dealt with by any one or set of panaceas, but can be treated effectively by transforming the organization into one with an internal market economy. The apparent need for downsizing and benchmarking is eliminated in such an economy. It dissolves the need to use TQM to improve quality and the need for process reengineering to increase productivity. Dissolving these needs is a lot better than trying to solve the problems they create.

Many of the problems panaceas address derive from the fact that most units within organizations do not obtain their income from those they serve but are subsidized from above. For example, personnel, finance, and data processing are units whose services are not normally paid for directly by the units they serve. They are budgeted from above out of funds obtained by taxing the units served, much like government agencies. There are two principal consequences. First, serving units are not nearly as responsive to those they serve as they are to those who subsidize them. Second, because they are subsidized monopolies they tend to bureaucratize. Bureaucracies tend to grow without limit because they believe that this provides maximum protection against downsizing. The fact is that they maximize the need for it because their principal mode of growth is to make work, work that has no useful product.

The need to downsize can virtually be eliminated by destroying internal bureaucratic monopolies, and this can be done by converting an enterprise's internal economy from one that is centrally planned and controlled into a market economy. At the national (macroeconomic) level we are dedicated to pursuit of a market economy as originally formulated by Adam Smith in his *Wealth of Nations*. But at the microeconomic level of the enterprise we usually employ the same kind of economic system as the Soviet Union used before its transformation—one that is centrally planned and controlled.

This inconsistency is often rationalized by reference to the difference in size between the nation state and even a large corporation. But this is nonsense. The Associated Press recently identified the twenty largest economies in the world, six of which were corporations. AT&T has a larger economy than a hundred nations.

Scale has nothing to do with it. The real reason for this inconsistency is that chief executives of our public and private institutions are not willing to give up their power over others. Unfortunately, we have learned that the more educated subordinates are, the less effective it is to use power as a means for getting them to do what one wants. To exercise power over someone is to command and control; to give power to someone is to *lead*.

    An internal market economy requires reduction of executive "power-over" but increases its "power-to," and it enables executives to manage systemically—that is, to manage the interactions of units rather than the units' actions taken separately. Without these changes it is, and will become, more and more difficult for enterprises to compete effectively in the increasingly turbulent and competitive global economy.

## An Internal Market Economy

What does a corporation look like that has transformed from a centrally planned and controlled economy to one that is based on a free market?

First, almost every unit, including the executive office, becomes a profit center. The exceptions are those units that, for one reason or another, cannot be permitted to serve external customers; for example, the corporate secretary and the corporate planning department. Such units are treated as cost centers but are assigned to profit centers.

The requirement that most units be profit centers does *not* mean that they must be profitable. For example, Corning has retained Steuben Glass despite its low profitability because it lends considerable prestige to the corporation. One university that employed an internal market economy retains its linguistic department despite the fact that its graduates are the most expensive for the university to turn out. The reason is that the department is one of the most prestigious in the world. On the other hand, departments that have been profitable but of low quality have been discontinued.

Although profitability is not necessarily required of every part of the enterprise, the profitability of each part is taken into account when evaluating its performance and considering how to treat it.

Second, each profit center is free to sell its output to whomever it wants, internally or externally, at whatever price it wants (subject to a few constraints described in the following two paragraphs). In addition, it can buy whatever it wants from whatever internal or external sources it wants. For example, a unit that needs accounting services can either buy them from an internal or external supplier, or provide them to itself. The same is true for data processing, other services, acquisitions of parts to be assembled, and even products.

These rules are subject to a few mild constraints. One is lawlike, intended to protect the ability of the enterprise to compete. For example, during the cold war IBM was prevented by the U.S. government from selling mainframe computers to the Soviet Union. A company that has a product based on a secret formula, like Coca-Cola, is not likely to permit its product to be made by an external producer.

The other type of constraint is specific rather than general: a corporate executive may override a particular lower-level decision to buy or sell a product or service from or to an external source. However, when this increases the cost or decreases the profitability of a transaction, the executive who does the overriding must compensate the unit affected for this loss. It is the executive's decision and he or she must pay for it. As overriding executives are also a profit centers, they must balance the cost of their overrides with the benefit their part of the organization obtains from them. In effect, the exercise of overrides is the management of interactions of units, not their separate actions.

Third, when an internal unit wants to buy something externally for which there is an internal supplier, the internal supplier is given the opportunity to bid for the order. However, the consuming unit is free to choose an external unit even if the internal supplier quotes a lower price. Price is not the only reason for selecting a supplier; other reasons are time to delivery, reliability, quality, and so on.

Asking for prices from external suppliers can create a problem that can and should be avoided. If one repeatedly asks them for quotes but never places an order with them, the sources may come to suspect that there is no possibility of a sale and therefore deliberately inflate the prices quoted. To avoid this, some business should be given to at least some of those asked to quote prices.

Fourth, one of the fundamental differences between a conventional organization and one employing an internal market economy is that every unit in the latter must pay for all services and supplies it receives, for rent of the space it occupies, and, most important, interest on the capital it employs either for operating or investment. Higher-level management acts like an investment bank for lower-level units. It provides capital but at a cost. This enables every unit to be evaluated using its return on the capital employed. Payment may be in the form of interest if the capital supplied is treated as a loan, or as dividends if the capital supplied is treated as stock ownership.

Fifth, units are permitted to accumulate profit up to a specified limit. The limit is set based on an estimate of the amount that the unit can invest at a return equal to or greater than what the higher-level unit can obtain. Up to that limit they can use the money accumulated however they see fit as long as it does not affect any other unit. If it does affect another unit, the affected unit must agree to the use or, if it doesn't, all the units affected together must go to the lowest level of management at which they converge for resolution of the difference—again, management of interactions.

Money accumulated above the limit goes to the next higher level of management, which pays interest on it to the unit from which it comes. This requirement elevates the status of "cash cows" that supply the enterprise with the capital it requires for development and growth.

## The Executive Office as a Profit Center

As noted earlier, the chief executive's office and the executive office of any business unit operate as profit centers. They incur costs for personnel, services, supplies, capital acquired by borrowing or investment, and costs of their overriding decisions. They derive income from the services and capital they provide units or dividends paid by them. Government taxes on corporate profit are allocated to units that are profit centers proportional to their contribution to that profit.

Because the executive office must also operate as a profit center, its costs tend to decrease dramatically under such a transformation. For example, when an internal market economy was introduced at Clark Equipment, its corporate overhead came down greatly because its headquarters shrank from about 450 people to about 50. Those displaced were reassigned to productive activities in subordinate units.

The requirement that the executive office operate as a profit center helps ensure that it sees itself as having a value-adding function. It makes executives conscious of the quality and responsiveness of their decisions and the services they provide. Furthermore, their dependence on the performance of subordinate units is made explicit and measurable.

## Examples

An increasing number of corporations have implemented internal markets successfully. I describe some of the more dramatic cases to illustrate the power of the concept.

### A Major Oil Company

This company had one of the largest computing facilities in the United States. Projections of the cost of computing showed that in a very few years the company would be spending more on computers than on people. The new CEO did not know whether this was good or bad. He asked my group if we could determine whether the money being spent on computing was justified. We naively said we thought we could.

We found that the computers were used mainly to prepare schedules for refineries and for the shipping of crude oil from the

Middle East to the refineries. We designed an evaluative experiment and went to discuss it with the refinery managers. We explained that some of these managers selected at random would be asked to prepare schedules manually while others would use the computer-generated schedules. They told us the latter was not possible because they never used the computer-produced schedules without modification. They explained that the model used by the computers left out some important qualitative variables that they had to take into account. Therefore, they always adjusted the computer-generated schedule given to them. We said that if we were given a record of their changes we might still be able to go ahead as planned. They told us that their changes were frequently made daily or within a day and no record of them was kept.

We learned much the same thing when we talked to those responsible for scheduling the shipping. After several months of complete frustration we found it impossible to evaluate the outputs of computing.

One day, out of desperation, we invoked Hitch's principle. Charley Hitch was a distinguished operations researcher at the RAND Corporation during and after World War II who eventually was demoted to presidency of the University of California. He once said, "If you can't solve the problem you're facing, you must be facing the wrong problem." We began to look for a different formulation of the problem.

Sure enough, when we reflected on what we were doing, we saw that we were trying to evaluate a product consumed by someone else. They were obviously better equipped to evaluate it than us. This led to a different formulation of the problem and different kind of proposed solution. We asked the CEO, "Why don't you make the corporate computing department a profit center? Let it charge its users whatever it wants for its services. But it should be free to solicit customers externally as well as internally. On the other hand, internal users should be free to use external computing services if they so desired." The CEO liked the proposal and implemented it.

In the next six months the computing center reduced the number of its computers by about half. Nevertheless, it continued to do almost all of the internal work because internal demand was significantly reduced once the users had to pay directly for the work they requested. The center still had time left over, which it began to sell to external users. Over time it generated a very profitable data-processing business while improving the quality and reducing the cost of its services. Such improvement and reduction were necessary if it was to attract and retain customers. The executive who had computer oversight responsibilities no longer had to be concerned with benchmarking the services provided; he had a much better way of evaluating it.

### An Electrical Equipment Manufacturer

A very good example of the power of an internal market economy, even though applied only to a part of a corporation, is provided by a large manufacturer of electrical and electronic equipment. One of its business units was a major manufacturer of small motors used mostly in large household appliances. A few very large manufacturers of such appliances bought most of its output. Another business unit supplied electrical wholesalers with replacement parts used primarily on production equipment. Included were small electric motors. The corporation's executives required the motor-producing unit to supply the other, and the other to use no other source of supply. As both units were profit centers, a transfer price for the motors was established. All hell broke loose.

The wholesaler-supply unit often needed electrical motors at a time when the producing unit was operating at capacity and preferred to supply its major customers who paid a higher price for the motors than the transfer price. Therefore, compliance with the corporate directive required it to sacrifice profit.

However, the wholesaler-supply unit was frequently offered equivalent motors by external manufacturers at a lower-than-transfer price. It could not buy them, thereby increasing its costs and lowering its profit.

Little wonder each unit hated the other. The intensity of this hate led to overt conflict that disrupted corporate activity and set a poor example for other units. The CEO asked us if we could find a way to reduce the conflict by adjusting the transfer price. We told him there was no such thing as a permanently fair transfer price, that sooner or later every transfer price would produce conflict. We suggested that he allow each unit to buy and sell wherever it wanted, but give the executive to which both units reported the ability to override these decisions. However, he should pay for the increased costs or lost profits incurred because of his overrides. The CEO agreed.

In the first year the executive responsible for oversight constrained the two business units to the tune of 3 million dollars. At the end of the year the corporate executive office met to evaluate this expenditure and decided it was not justified; it bought no tangible synergy. The constraints were removed the following year. Profitability of both business units and the corporation were increased and the conflict between the units was eliminated. They became completely cooperative.

## An Ivy League University

As indicated earlier, a major university applied an internal market economy to its departments. As a result two unprofitable and less-than-high-quality units were discontinued, but one unprofitable unit was retained because of its prestige. However, the major effect of this transformation was on the behavior of other departments. Previously, growth had been the major objective of almost all the departments because they took stability to be positively correlated with size. But now, for the first time, they had to worry about the effects of size on their profitability. Unconstrained growth no longer appeared to be an effective means to their ends.

In one department, faculty members were treated as profit centers. Their income was associated with the number of student credits their teaching produced and the amount of billable research in which they engaged. A faculty member who did not end up the year in the black could not receive an increase in salary. Professors were amazed when they learned how much teaching they had to do to break even. For example, each academic year a full professor had to teach five courses of thirty-seven students each in order to break even. Before the new economy was installed most were teaching only two seminars per year with an average of about eight students in each. Their orientation toward teaching and research changed abruptly.

Professors now wanted to teach large first-year required courses in order to earn enough to enable them to conduct their advanced seminars without sacrificing future income. Contractual research was no longer viewed as academic prostitution. Competition for grants and contracts increased dramatically and participation in research was much easier to obtain.

## Internal Markets in the Public Sector

The use of an internal market economy is by no means restricted to private for-profit organizations. It can be, and has been, used effectively by government. For example, the use of educational vouchers, suggested by Christopher Jenks of Harvard University and publicized by Milton Friedman, involves a conversion to a market economy. In this system schools receive income by cashing in vouchers obtained from students who have a choice of public schools to attend. The vouchers are supplied by government. They can also be used to pay all or part of the tuition required by nonreligious private schools. This system requires schools to compete in order to survive and this, in turn, requires they be responsive to the needs of those they service.

In one version of the voucher system, every public school must accept all applicants from the area for which they are responsible. Students from the area who are accepted at and attend schools in different areas must be compensated for their transportation costs by the schools in the areas in which they live. In such a system if schools are required to select at random from among applicants living outside their area, segregation in schools becomes a nonissue.

To take another example, a large centralized licensing bureau in Mexico City had a terrible record of inefficiency and poor service. It was divided into small offices that were placed in each section of the city. These offices were compensated for each license they issued; they had no other source of income. Those who wanted a license could use any of the offices. Unlike the centralized bureaucratic monopoly they replaced, the small offices could only survive by providing good service inexpensively. Service time decreased, the quality of service increased, and the corruption that had previously permeated the service virtually disappeared.

It should be noted that privatizing a public service does not necessarily convert it to a market economy. Privatization can preserve a monopoly, which is antithetical to a market economy in which competition is essential.

## Objections to an Internal Market Economy

Proposals for the introduction of an internal market economy are usually received with four types of concern.

First, skeptics argue that the additional amount of accounting required would be horrendous. Not true! The amount of accounting required is actually reduced. Most of the accounting currently required of organizational units is done to facilitate control by higher-level organizational units. In an internal market economy, however, only profit-and-loss statements and balance sheets need to be provided to others in the organization. Any additional information they request should be paid for by them. This has a strong tendency to reduce the amount of unnecessary accounting information flowing within organizations, particularly up.

Second, some argue that an internal market economy will increase conflict and competition between parts of the organization. Again, not true! Transfer pricing, which is a surrogate for market pricing in a centrally planned and controlled economy, produces intense internal conflict and competition. Peter Drucker once observed that there is more competition within firms than between them, and it is a lot less ethical.

*A capsule of int. market idea*

Most organizational units have much better relations with external suppliers that they choose than with internal suppliers that they can't select. The competition stimulated by an internal market economy is between external and internal suppliers of the same goods or services, not between internal supplying and supplied units. Moreover, internal suppliers who must compete with external suppliers for internal customers are much more responsive to their customers' needs than monopolistic internal suppliers.

Consider the case of a large food producer that had a substantial market research unit, a monopolistic subsidized supplier of its services to other organizational units. It was held in low regard by its users because it was considered unresponsive and inferior to outside market research organizations. Corporate management converted it into a profit center, permitted it to market its services externally, and its users to obtain market research services externally. Using units were required to pay for whatever services they used whatever the source. All internal users initially moved to external suppliers, forcing the internal supplier to look for external work. It eventually succeeded but only after it had significantly improved the quality of its services. It became a thriving business. Internal units began to wonder why it was so successful and tried it out. This time they found it responsive and competent. Internal demand became so great that the market research unit had to turn down some work offered by external organizations.

Third, some argue that an internal market economy cannot be installed in one part of an organization, only in the whole. This, it is claimed, may be very difficult if not impossible. Difficult, yes, but not impossible! About three years ago one of a company's two manufacturing arms converted to an internal market economy. The containing company was not willing to adopt the same type of economy. Therefore, the division had to operate as a market-oriented unit within a centrally planned and controlled economy.

The containing company continued to charge the division for all corporately provided services through an overhead allocation. The division could not break these charges down into those for services it received and those it didn't. Therefore, the unit developed surrogate costs for the services it received and treated unaccounted-for charges from the company as a tax. It continued to report to the corporation in the conventional way but operated with two sets of books.

One year after its conversion, the division's effectiveness had increased so much that the corporation and other parts of it began to wonder what was happening. When the corporation found out, it did not convert to a similar system but it changed the information required of and provided to the division. This enabled it to operate more easily with its internal market economy. Other units subsequently followed suit.

A similar case involved the R&D unit of Esso Petroleum Canada. It also converted to an internal market economy within a centrally controlled corporate economy. But in this case the parent company tried to facilitate the conversion because it was considered to be a trial that could lead to a similar transformation in other units, and possibly the whole corporation.

Fourth, some do not seriously consider an internal market economy because they maintain that certain internal service functions cannot "reasonably" be expected to attract external customers. Accounting and human-resource departments are frequently cited as examples. One corporation headquartered in the Midwest converted both these departments into profitable business units. Many local small- and medium-sized businesses that could not afford internal accounting and human-resource services of high quality welcomed the availability of such services.

Another company that occupied a number of buildings in a suburb of a major city converted its facilities-and-services department (buildings, grounds, and utilities) into a profit center that operated within a corporate internal market economy. All of its internal users shifted to external suppliers from whom they obtained better services at a lower cost. As a result, the facilities-and-services department gradually shrank and eventually was eliminated with a considerable saving to the company.

## More Advantages of an Internal Market Economy

*A*
*Capsule*
*of*
*the*
*benefits*

A number of the benefits of an internal market economy have already been identified—in particular, increased responsiveness of internal suppliers, better quality and reduced cost of internally supplied services and products, continual right-sizing, debureaucratization, and so on. A few other advantages are worth mentioning.

First, because almost every corporate unit operating within an internal market economy becomes a profit center, similar measures of performance can be applied to all of them. This makes it possible to compare the performance of units that were previously not comparable, for example, manufacturing and accounting.

Second, managers of profit centers within an internal market are necessarily general managers of semiautonomous business units. This provides them with opportunities to acquire, improve, and display their general management skills. Therefore, executives are better able to evaluate the general management ability of their subordinates.

Third, when units are converted to profit centers and are given the autonomy that goes with it, their managers are in a much better position to obtain all the information they require to manage well. They become more concerned with providing themselves with the information they need than with providing their superiors with the information they want.

―――――

Conversion to an internal market economy obviously raises a number of difficult issues. Therefore, it is not a task to be undertaken lightly or by the fainthearted. The conversion requires courageous managers, *transformational leaders*. The potential payoff, however, is an order-of-magnitude increase in effectiveness. The transformation of corporations into internal market economies, corporate perestroika, is as important to our country on the microeconomic level as it was to the Soviet Union on the macroeconomic level.

# 3

# Reintroducing Alcoa to Economic Reality

## John P. Starr

Since the dawn of time, parents have had an irrepressible instinct to protect their young. It may sound a bit strange, but corporate managers often suffer from this same instinct. We carefully insulate our "babies," the departments that support any organization, from the harsh realities of the outside world.

In the past, when national boundaries limited competition, we could afford this protective behavior. We often used our collective strength to support weak departments that might not be able to stand on their own. For many years, U.S. auto companies supported subsidiaries that utilized outdated technology and production processes and produced inferior quality. Under the pressure of global competition, however, other manufacturers required their suppliers to grow and compete vigorously. The result was that these firms set today's high standards of productivity and quality, which in turn enabled them to dominate their industries.

In a different sense, these fierce competitors were really better parents because they required their youngsters to grow up into

---

John P. Starr spent twenty-one years as a manager at Alcoa Corporation. He was president of the Alcoa Separations Technology division at the time of the reorganization described in this chapter. Starr is currently the owner of Cheyenne Canyon Inn in Colorado.

responsible adults. Protecting departments in organizations can lead to the same problems confronting any parent who is overprotective of its young. Sooner or later the child must face the world, and, if he or she is unprepared, some aggressor is likely to threaten when the child is out of the parent's sight. To avoid the business equivalent of being eaten alive, all of our units must be required to become fully capable, mature enterprises that can survive and prosper in the real world against tough competition.

## Weaning Support Units at Alcoa Separations Technology

Alcoa, like so many other corporations in U.S. industry, was once comfortably ensconced in its cozy, protected world. We were in a growing industry, and we had strong technical and commercial positions that allowed ample opportunities to make money. Not surprisingly, whenever operating costs would rise, sales and marketing teams were dispatched to raise prices. Things were looking pretty good.

However, the outside world started to change. Competitors became more skillful and technical gaps began to close. Perhaps of greatest importance, our past success had brought growth, and this growth caused some of the large departments to lose contact with their customers. Many of these departments had become more driven by their own bureaucratic internal processes than by the need to deliver solutions to demanding customers.

Within this envelope of Alcoa Corporation, Alcoa Separations was a $100-million-plus subsidiary that had been assembled by adding several acquired businesses to an existing base within the company. Its primary business was making engineered equipment and systems, particularly for the water and waste treatment industries. This equipment usually consists of large tanks connected by complex piping arrangements, with numerous valves and fittings scattered throughout to control flow.

This is roughly the way our organization worked—like a cumbersome, mechanical plumbing system. Groups functioned as "towers of power." Communications between units were highly formal, much like the flow of liquid through pipes in the equipment they made—limited to a few tightly controlled, precise directions. There was little room for creativity and considerable filtering of customer input at many stages in the process. Many departments were far more interested in what went on inside their own "tank" than in what happened to the customer at the output end of the process.

As a result, groups were optimizing their own activities at the cost of suboptimizing results for the whole system. In comparing the performance of our departments against competitive standards, we found that a number of units were seriously falling behind. They were losing the advantages of speed, flexibility, and customer contact that had driven success in their smaller, more entrepreneurial days. Comfortable growth and compartmentalization had begun to insulate departments from reality.

Like all good parents who wish the best for their children's future, we had to wean these indulged youngsters if they were to survive in a harsh competitive world.

## Switching to an Internal Market System

This unflattering portrait of our unwieldy structure led to a decision to recapture the customer- and market-driven forces that had created the group's success in the first place. We felt a need to refocus our efforts through a system that would require each unit to constantly examine its activities and goals against competitive benchmarks of quality, cost, and customer satisfaction. After much reflection, we decided to follow the model of an internal market system.

In this system, the input units of manufacturing, engineering, and R&D are viewed as suppliers to the business units, which are then treated as their customers. The business units in turn serve their internal customers, the sales units, which provide the final output to the environment. The idea is that everyone in the organization has a customer and a supplier, and in turn is itself a customer or a supplier. Just as in real-world situations, suppliers must develop sound working relationships with their customers and raise the quality of their goods and services to compete with other vendors. Customers are free to choose among possible suppliers, both internal and external, so internal vendors who do not perform could be replaced by external suppliers, the equivalent of contracting out an operation. The flip side is that the internal suppliers also have the opportunity to seek outside clients for their goods and services.

If your organization is like ours, however, achieving this goal is easier said than done. When we originally discussed the concept, all our people who were in the customer role literally licked their chops. At long last, they said, they would have the freedom to dump those rascals down the hall who were really causing all their problems. And those in a supplier mode said, Aha! Just let our internal customers try finding an outside vendor who will put up with the same pitifully poor information we've been dealing with. Maybe, just maybe, this could make our salespeople shape up and give us what we really need to perform well.

Obviously, we could not tolerate a situation where all parts of the organization were allowed to jump ship, which would have allowed chaos to reign supreme. To make the transition in orderly fashion, we agreed to establish transfer prices based on the previous year's costs. Each unit would use these prices for a specified period without having their customers move to external suppliers or having their suppliers abandon them for better customers. During this warm-up period, suppliers would be expected to take whatever actions necessary to bring their costs and quality up to competitive standards and customers would be expected to clean up their act by collaborating with supplier groups to help lower their costs.

As this process proceeded, we found that some of our units apparently could not compete with costs quoted from outside vendors. I say apparently because our cost system had never been designed to give accurate breakdowns by department, with overhead properly applied as if each department were a company in its own right. Quite often, the costs for a given unit did not delineate fixed corporate expenses that would not go away if a particular piece of business were given to an outside supplier.

The hidden effect of these "membership" costs is nicely illustrated by a story about a chain of food stores. Several of the stores were not profitable, so the company decided to close them. After doing so, they reallocated corporate overhead to the remaining stores, which increased their costs and made a few more stores unprofitable. They then closed these additional stores and reallocated again, without seeing where all this was heading. It took a while to realize how important such membership costs can be if not addressed in a meaningful context.

This problem was especially acute in our case because we were moving to an internal market system. We had to spend a considerable amount of time and effort to reclassify these fixed overhead costs so that comparisons to outside vendors would be accurate. This is a crucial task in the transition to a market economy. Without a workable, responsive cost analysis system, inappropriate competitive comparisons are likely. If this happens, the market approach will not work well. The process bogs down and comparisons become meaningless.

Other difficulties arose after costs were refigured along these lines. A lot of effort was wasted by managers arguing about the relative fairness of cost figures rather than addressing the underlying competitive issues that were being raised. People also complained vigorously about the level of the transfer prices in general, which pointed to other problems.

These were transient issues, however, because they occurred directly out of our decision to curtail complete market freedom somewhat during the transition phase. When the market system was fully implemented, we simply allowed the price offerings of competitors to guide internal transactions. In the final analysis, there is nothing to argue about in a market system. If you don't like the terms offered, it is always possible to take your business elsewhere.

It took us far longer than we had hoped to proceed down this path, primarily because our financial system was weaker than many of us had suspected. We had to relearn the first rule of management: you can only manage something if you can measure it. Unfortunately, we found ourselves woefully short on our capability of measuring various operations to the level that a market economy requires. As a result, our ability to capture many of the benefits of the concept were delayed.

We know now that these financial measurement problems existed long before we embarked on the market economy approach. One of the unexpected benefits of the internal market system was to make this shortcoming visible. After improving our information systems we were able to take the corrective actions needed to make each unit more competitive and to optimize overall results for the entire company. I cannot too strongly emphasize how critical solid financial analysis is early in the process to make an internal market system work.

## Evolution of the Internal Market Structure

Our experience with the internal market system produced both successes and failures. Perhaps our most dramatic success has come from, of all places, our research and development department. Under the old system, the only way R&D could fund projects was to convince a business unit that it had a great idea. As a result, the battles between R&D and business units became legendary. R&D always complained that the marketing groups were too short-term oriented and did not understand the complexities of long-term development. Business units complained that R&D could never finish anything, was prohibitively expensive, and was always off working on some harebrained idea rather than accomplishing projects that would yield revenue some time in this century.

After the internal market was working, R&D was forced to do some serious reflection. Realizing that internal customers had limited funds and no desire for long-term work, it decided to reorient itself to focus on various hot projects emerging from the business units. This did not satisfy its interests in more creative and challenging projects, so it also decided to search outside for funding from various clients that valued its special expertise. Certain boundaries were placed on this pursuit, primarily that any work obtained must be linked to the strategic direction of the company.

As a result of these efforts, almost 35 percent of R&D's budget was funded via external sources. It did an exceptional job of finding funding for projects that contribute to our strategic goals, and even the business units were pleasantly surprised by the new possibilities that have been introduced. This contact with outside clients has also shown that R&D costs were not as far out of line with competitive pricing as we had thought.

There have been other success stories as well. Our manufacturing organization decided to subcontract several operations that could be performed better and more cheaply by outside vendors, at great savings in time and money. The European sales division moved aggressively to represent additional product lines from other divisions and suppliers where they could add value. And our engineering unit created several subcontractor relationships to help meet customer schedules during peak periods.

But we also had to struggle in some areas. The most crucial problem occurred where it was least expected—in our business units, which package and market our products. They envisioned the new system as their personal nirvana, an ideal world in which they were the customer supreme and could force their internal suppliers to meet every whim. These demands were enforced by the threat of taking their business elsewhere if they did not get action.

The business units could have prevailed in their demands if they had been able to meet outside competition by serving their clients' needs effectively. Unfortunately, some marketing managers took a myopic view and forced outdated policies and procedures on their captive internal suppliers, blocking many of the quality and cost improvements that might have been possible.

With 20–20 hindsight, we can now see that the move to an internal market revealed the wastefulness of these antiquated processes, just as it showed the truth about our financial system. We did not realize how uncompetitive we were until the new demand for accountability forced the problem to surface. To use my earlier analogy of manager as parent, we had left an unprotected child in a dangerous situation.

Ironically, the very units that were used to dealing with external customers disavowed the checks and balances of internal competition. That development truly caught us off guard, and highlights how crucial market forces are for keeping every part of the organization alert.

Ultimately, we were able to address this flaw by focusing on external customer satisfaction as the common measure driving performance throughout the company. This was accomplished by forcing all units to benchmark their own processes and to bring them up to leading standards. This, in turn, drove the need to restructure operations and retrain people; but even with ample training opportunities we lost some people who could not adapt to a competitive environment. Now, however, the organization has a solid base of knowledge and tools to upgrade our marketing by linking improvements across the organization to the customer.

## Revitalization

A sense of revitalization grew as the internal market system drove accountability for performance into all layers and units of the organization. This accountability can be viewed as a chain linking all successive internal customer dealings to the ultimate needs of the final customer. It also relies heavily on monitoring and measuring performance at each step in this chain. The net effect is a continuous striving for improvement and excellence in all we do.

We have had particular success where this process has been pushed all the way to the factory floor. In several work centers, we gave teams the freedom to rearrange their equipment to gain better work flow of material. Later, we also allowed them the authority to control their own work-in-process inventory.

One of the most far-reaching changes was to have workers receive orders directly from their customers via computers that we installed in the work centers. Previously, supervisors were needed to transfer this planning information to work centers and to provide instructions at the beginning of each workday. The supervisor would then check back during the day to see if people were working on the proper jobs at the proper pace. Under the new system, the work team takes this planning information directly and schedules its own work to meet customer demands.

With this new flexibility, a direct link to their customers, and feedback on the profitability of their units, members of the work centers became highly interested, even excited, about their jobs in a way they never had been before. Having their destiny in their own hands, work teams could directly see the result of their actions on costs and on how quickly a product moved out the door. As a result, lead times for moving products through one work center were reduced from between twelve and fourteen weeks to between two and five days. The team is confident it can further reduce this to four hours as it totally closes the loop with customers and suppliers.

One major result of this self-organizing approach is that far fewer supervisors are needed, permitting layers to be removed from the organizational hierarchy. Those supervisors remaining act more like coaches and champions of continuous improvement. The company is clearly heading toward self-managed teams that are driven directly by customer demands and accountable for final performance. In short, they are becoming autonomous work teams that behave as small business enterprises in their own right.

During the next year, additional units continued to implement the internal market concept, thereby driving accountability, competitiveness, and rigorous financial discipline within each operating unit, and leading to significant gains in productivity and performance. Most notably, output per worker in the water treatment and environmental segments nearly doubled. Also, lead times were cut by up to 80 percent in the water treatment segment, resulting in a more profitable and dynamic business.

Today, this business is a successful part of the rapidly growing U.S. Filter Corporation, which acquired it from Alcoa in 1992. U.S. Filter is one of the country's largest companies dedicated to fluid processing equipment and technology, contributing a further customer focus on critical items for success within this business. Meanwhile, Alcoa continues to refocus on its core aluminum business and is attempting to drive the same concepts of accountability, quality, and customer satisfaction throughout all of its businesses.

## Hopes for the Future

Improvements of this type represent only a small start to what is possible. Give people the freedom to pursue their own good ideas in an environment of trust and cooperation, with timely measurement and feedback on how they are doing, and progress is sure to be made. We may not make quantum leaps, but the results nonetheless produce impressive, constant gains.

Going back to my analogy about parents and managers again, seldom does a baby move directly from his or her first spoken words to delivering the State of the Union Address before Congress. What we experience in life, and what we should attempt to emulate in business, is a series of incremental steps that keep improving our capability to tackle ever more challenging tasks by a never-ending process of learning.

The best way to bring learning alive in our organizations is to introduce market-based concepts into each and every job and group in the corporation. If we desire to have our organizations function at higher levels of performance, we must gradually expose them to an environment of free enterprise. There is a lot of discretionary effort out there in capable people who want to perform. It is just waiting to be tapped by managers with vision.

A market-based economy operating in competition allows organizations and people to grow and mature. Just as nature can transform weak, helpless children into powerful adults able to protect their parents, so can small business units become strong internal enterprises able to strengthen the parent corporation as a whole. Our challenge as managers is to harness people's great reserves of dormant energy by turning them loose in a market-based enterprise system.

Alcoa's experience in moving to an internal market system has proven to be a valuable lesson in good corporate parenting. It has forcefully driven home the need to stop protecting indulged units, and instead to teach them how to cope in the real world. Only by learning to survive in a competitive environment can we hope to produce stable, productive, long-term business relationships. Insulating individuals from such hard but unavoidable realities inevitably produces unproductive, unstable situations that cannot long endure, whether in nature or in business.

# 4

# Market-Based Management at Koch Industries

## Wayne Gable

The command model of organization has dominated business for decades, just as the command model of economics dominated centrally planned economies. It is no accident that Lenin was a great admirer of Frederick Taylor, the father of scientific management who was one of the builders of the hierarchical corporation. In fact, Lenin designed portions of the Soviet economy after Taylor's model of American business. And conversely, Taylor thought communism was a great social advance.

The reason for this mutual admiration is that both centrally planned economies and hierarchical corporations are based on the same concept: centralized control. This lesson derived from comparing organizations and economies underlies the philosophy that has inspired Koch Industries to develop what we call *market-based management*.[1] Market-based management uses the concepts of free

---

Wayne Gable is director of government relations at Koch Industries. He holds a Ph.D. in economics from George Mason University and has served in a variety of positions at Koch. Koch is not well known because the company is privately held by the Koch family, but it is the second-largest private corporation in the United States, with annual revenues of $24 billion. The company is headquartered in Wichita, Kansas, and operates petroleum, chemical, agricultural, and financial service operations all over the world.

enterprise rather than hierarchy to structure and manage an organization. We think this philosophy is especially important today because of the following central facts:

1. Managers are searching for a new model of organization.

2. The effective use of knowledge is the key to creating this new model.

3. Market-based management offers a superior way to handle knowledge.

It is clear now that the old command-and-control form of organization no longer works. The original thought was that a cadre of well-trained, competent managers would be selected to run the enterprise, and they would use sophisticated planning systems to do this in a rational manner that ensures optimal solutions. This was an elegant idea, and it still holds the attention of many people.

But the collapse of communism, the decline of AT&T, GM, and IBM, and the disenchantment with big government has demonstrated that the concept of command-and-control management is seriously flawed. Friedrich Hayek called it the "fatal conceit," the belief that leaders or technical experts know what is best for others and that they can more effectively manage large organizations while ignoring what most people know or think.[2]

## The Koch Philosophy

Koch Industries sought to remedy this problem as Charles Koch, our chairman and CEO, led the company toward unusual success. During the past twenty-five years the firm has enjoyed a hundred–fold increase in revenues while the number of employees rose from seven hundred to thirteen thousand. People often ask us, "How did you achieve this remarkable growth?"

The usual explanations cannot explain such achievements. We do not own more or better assets, nor are we smarter than our competitors. We are convinced that Koch's performance is largely attributable to the dynamic features of our unique management philosophy—market-based management.

The development of this philosophy was challenging but fairly straightforward because it was guided by our present knowledge of free market economies. Charles Koch and his associates simply applied the best features of free-enterprise principles to the management of corporations. Table 4.1 outlines the six systems that compose this philosophy.

This framework draws heavily on lessons learned from using "market process analysis" to understand how free markets work in society. That is, we study how markets facilitate economic growth through complex interactions. To provide a comparable framework for organizations, market-based management focuses on the most critical elements of the free market system and identifies parallels in management practice, as shown in Table 4.1. Implementing these six market-based management systems can bring the power of free markets inside a company to create a spontaneous form of organizational activity and growth. Here are brief descriptions of these key systems.

The *Mission System* helps a company identify what the organization must do well to succeed in its industry and competitive environment. This includes defining its core competencies and comparative advantages that are typically part of competitive strategy.

**Table 4.1. Six Key Systems in Market Economies and Market Organizations**

| Market Economy | Market Organization |
|---|---|
| Comparative advantage | Corporate mission |
| Rules of just conduct | Values and culture |
| Property rights | Roles and responsibilities |
| Market incentives | Compensation and motivation |
| Free flow of ideas | Generation and use of knowledge |
| Price system | Internal markets |

*(handwritten annotation: Parallels to the free market system (lft. side))*

The Mission System also encourages development of what Peter Drucker called a "theory of the business" as well as a thorough understanding of the firm's customers and markets.

The power of a clearly defined, market-based mission can be seen in Koch's acquisition of the United Gas Pipeline Company in 1992. United was in bankruptcy proceedings because it had been managed as a utility in the gas transmission business without focusing on the effective use of its resources to create value and serve customer needs. Upon buying the company, Koch immediately implemented a mission focusing its unique resources on delivering customer service. Within five years the company ranked among the most profitable and efficient gas systems in North America—even while remaining in a regulated industry.

A company's *Values and Culture* provide the guidelines and norms that influence the decisions and actions of its employees. Having well-established values allows everyone to fully comprehend and live by certain shared understandings; it fosters an environment of trust, mutual respect, intellectual honesty, and open communications, which in turn encourages cooperation, risk taking, and innovation.

A well-defined system of *Roles and Responsibilities* is critical for establishing clear accountability for both organizational units and individual employees. When linked to rewards, clearly defined roles and responsibilities encourage employees to develop a sense of personal ownership for their share of the company's objectives, rather than to just do a job. Market-based management also recommends developing key measures of success which link accountability to profitability. Finally, employees must have appropriate authority to achieve the results for which they are accountable.

In a free market, profit and loss indicate the extent to which resources are used efficiently and value is added, as well as providing incentives for improvement. Similarly, the company's *Compensation and Motivation* system can provide financial and intrinsic incentives that reward employees for contributing to business performance. This system usually includes allowing employees to share in the financial benefits of their efforts through some form of incentive pay.

A company can do its best job of identifying opportunities, solving problems, and making decisions only by utilizing the best knowledge available within the organization. Much of this knowledge is dispersed among employees (local), difficult to articulate (tacit), and unproven. The four key systems just described encourage linking appropriate employee knowledge with responsibilities. The *Generation and Use of Knowledge* system helps management understand such linkages and generate knowledge critical to the company's mission.

A good example of using knowledge effectively is provided by Koch's oil refinery in Corpus Christi, Texas. A study of operations found forty thousand barrels of product in the bottoms of tanks that were inaccessible because discharge lines were three feet above the tank bottoms. This was like finding a new room in your home that you could not use. A team of marketing, operations, engineering, and accounting people redesigned the tanks to gain access to the forty thousand barrels, worked with customers to find a use for this additional product, and converted the refinery to the new system. Discovering and coordinating the sharing of this diverse knowledge on refinery operations, customer demands, and tank redesign thus transformed wasted oil into profitable new business that served an unmet need.

Finally, the *Internal Markets* system uses many features of free market systems within the company. Prices summarize a vast amount of information about the relative scarcity of and demand for resources. Establishing prices for products and services that employees use daily provides them with crucial information they have no other way of obtaining. Employees who understand the profitability of their organization and have the authority to make business decisions are able to use this knowledge to make more informed buying decisions.

## Implementing the Philosophy

When these six systems function successfully within a company, organizational learning occurs; the company continuously finds more effective ways to mobilize the knowledge and creativity of its employees to achieve its mission and to improve its financial results.

This capability will become more critical to business success as more companies realize that, whether they are in service or manufacturing industries, they are also in the knowledge business. The key to understanding the advantages of our system is the realization that knowledge is now the most critical strategic factor in any business.

Further, the most valuable form of knowledge often consists of tacit knowledge, the personal understanding that resides in people. Tacit knowledge cannot be transferred easily because it is so idiosyncratic. For example, it is almost impossible for a bike rider to explain this skill adequately to others who have never experienced the unique feel of riding a bicycle.

And with the onset of a knowledge-based economy, this means that it is now almost impossible to manage organizations effectively using command principles. Top managers often do not possess the intimate understanding of business processes, customer needs, difficult problems, personal skills, and other forms of tacit knowledge residing in their employees. The fact is that much, if not most, of the valuable skills and understanding needed to make sensible business decisions is inherently a highly personal form of knowledge dispersed locally among many diverse people throughout the organization. The only good solution is to move the decision-making process to that point where the knowledge resides, thereby creating a decentralized, free enterprise form of management.

The market model is also essential because freely established prices for the internal transfer of goods and services carry valuable information needed to manage a corporate economy. By defining all units as internal enterprises held accountable for their financial performance and free to operate as they think best, the corporation benefits by ensuring that resources are put to their best use, that units produce value, and that improvements in economic performance are rewarded.

This point was driven home to me in particular when the group I work for faced the need to transfer these concepts into hard practice. The Koch government relations office in Washington, D.C., had always thought of itself as a service function, so we tried to help other Koch units, add value to their operations, evaluate our performance, and minimize our costs, and we were rewarded based on how well we did. However, it was one thing to convince the CEO that we were doing well and quite another to convince the units we served—our true internal customers—that they should pay for our services out of their bottom line. To say the least, this transition had a huge impact on the attitudes of the government relations group, our values, and our guiding incentives.

One could argue about the merits of this particular arrangement, but the main point it illustrates is the enormous power that market mechanisms can unleash to guide organizational behavior in new directions. Most of the normal management tools—annual performance evaluations, hiring and training competent people, strong leadership, and the like—pale in significance when compared to the economic effects of market forces.

This does not mean that Koch managers are antagonistic toward the use of TQM, reengineering, or the many other concepts that have become popular recently. Rather, we have found that these and almost all other management tools work better when they are used within a market-based framework. By analyzing, testing, and improving on these ideas, we are better able to discern which concepts truly add value and then apply them in a more useful manner. This also helps us avoid the "flavor of the month" syndrome that plagues so many companies.

The power of market-based management can pose a challenge at times because it can easily produce negative consequences. When Koch first moved to its market system, a sense of cost-consciousness immediately pervaded many units, often producing distorted behavior. For instance, some managers began cutting costs on critical programs, such as maintenance and safety, in order to enhance their short-term performance. This is the classic problem of trading off short-term benefits for long-term performance, and so it was necessary to remind people of the danger. The goal of business should be to improve long-term value, and it may be necessary to revise incentive systems to reflect this need.

When implemented properly, however, this approach can also improve operations dramatically. For example, the accounting department initially suffered a serious problem when many business units stopped using and paying for its services. It turned out that the monthly reports accounting had provided for many years were being routinely thrown out because they were useless to operating managers. Obviously this caused a lot of heartburn to our accountants. But they met with their now-paying clients to discuss the problem and learned that they really needed other types of accounting information. After accounting revised its reporting systems, the problem was solved.

Please note that the market process served a valuable role here by bringing out a serious problem that had gone undetected for years. Once again, the value of economic accountability, market pricing, freedom in choosing suppliers, and similar factors is seen to lie in the ability of markets to provide essential information.

This approach has proven so valuable that it has been extended to all line operations and to most staff units as well. Business units are treated as profit centers, held accountable for their performance but free to manage their operations as they think best. Also, accounting, training, government relations, information services, legal services, environmental compliance, and a variety of other support functions are provided to line units on a market basis in which unit managers may choose to purchase the service or not. Even the CEO's office has been operated as a profit center.

Because of this clear focus on accountability, the company benefits in many other ways. For instance, it has allowed us to abolish centrally approved budgets. In place of command-and-control budgeting, Koch tries to approximate a market's allocation mechanisms. Managers and employees who perform well are accorded greater resources and discretion, and vice versa.

*[handwritten margin note: This seems sensible. when you have regular budgeting, then the task becomes to spend all the budget to keep your budget level up and increasing?]*

## The Need for a Market Framework of Management

Let me conclude by putting the experiences of our company in a broader perspective.

The failure of command economies is surely one of the most powerful lessons to be learned from this century. The massive changes occurring now are more fundamental, more rapid, and more potentially devastating than at any time since the Industrial Revolution. Our present world faces a comparable revolution that will redefine the role of corporations, governments, entire industries, managers, and employees. Change of this magnitude is the most difficult process a corporation can undertake, but it is can also be the most rewarding.

To move ahead with clarity we need far more than the management techniques being used currently. Without a broader conceptual framework that is appropriate for the unique conditions of an emerging knowledge economy, these tools are likely to prove disappointing, conflicting, and misleading.

*[handwritten margin note: emerging knowledge economy.]*

The greatest need of modern managers is to develop a new philosophy of management based on principles of enterprise rather than hierarchy. That is the value of the system we have developed at Koch Industries. The power of this system has only been partially tapped even by companies like ours that have been working on it for many years, so the challenges and opportunities to improve on this basic idea are enormous.

*[handwritten margin note: need to create a learning org.]*

We suggest that our experience offers an example of the type of organization that can be developed throughout the business community. Obviously, each firm has to apply these ideas in its own way to suit its special needs and values. But we believe that the coming decades will see the management paradigm of hierarchy replaced by a new paradigm based on principles of enterprise and markets.

## Notes

1. The term *market-based management* is copyrighted © by Koch Industries.

2. Friedrich Hayek, *The Fatal Conceit* (University of Chicago Press, 1990).

# 5

# Lufthansa Soars on Internal Markets

## Mark Lehrer

The airline industry has never been an easy arena to compete in, but the task of airline managers was made even more difficult in the 1980s and 1990s by deregulation, market turbulence, and technological change. One of Lufthansa's top managers put the dilemma as follows: "We are used to thinking in terms of certainty and safety for passengers and production. But the competitive environment has become unstable and uncertain. This results in a dialectic. We produce safety and certainty for our passengers, but not for the career prospects of our managers. We have had to give up the promotions of past eras in which managers were guaranteed an automatic climb up the corporate ladder. Now it's more a matter of individual initiative."

In 1995, Lufthansa instituted an internal market system in order to master this complex challenge. As a result, the passenger, cargo,

---

Mark Lehrer is a Research Fellow at the Social Science Center Berlin. His recent Ph.D. dissertation (INSEAD, 1997) deals with competition among European flag carriers. He has published several articles applying the theory of comparative political economy to strategic management. This chapter draws extensively on two INSEAD case studies written by the author with Professor Heinz Thanheiser, *Lufthansa: The Turnaround* (INSEAD, 1995) and *Internal Markets at Lufthansa* (INSEAD, in preparation, title subject to change), as well as Lufthansa's annual reports.

maintenance, and data processing divisions of Lufthansa are now legally separate units that transact business with one another as customers and suppliers.

## Turning the Company Around

Lufthansa's internal markets actually come at the tail end of an exciting turnaround process. Since the European Commission began its liberalization of European civil aviation in 1987, there have been clear winners and losers among Europe's national flag carriers. "Aided" by the Gulf War and excess capacity in the 1990s, Europe's aviation authorities did succeed in creating a truly competitive market for aviation services. So competitive, in fact, that without the injection of state aid a large number of the national carriers would no longer be solvent. While the liberalized market drove a visible performance wedge between the stronger and weaker carriers, one national carrier managed to find the inner strength to move without state aid into the winners category. This was Lufthansa.

On the brink of financial disaster in 1992, Lufthansa managed an astounding turnaround that enabled it to post record profits in 1994 and 1995. Its CEO, Jürgen Weber, became a household name in Europe. The turnaround was a bloodless cultural revolution, a corporate-wide team effort during which the phrase "mental change" (in English!) became a permanent fixture in Lufthansa's corporate vocabulary. In a spurt of organizational energy and brainstorming, costs were sharply reduced, operations were restructured, and the company strategically repositioned itself from being the German flag carrier to being the European anchor of a global alliance that included United, Thai, SAS, and other regional airlines. Thanks in part to the indefatigable Weber's series of "town meetings" with Lufthansa employees all over the globe, Lufthansa was able to realize major productivity improvements and personnel reductions through voluntary departures without a strike.

## Planning the New Corporate Structure

By late 1993 Lufthansa's efforts had put it out of the danger zone—for the short term. But Weber and his colleagues knew that in the longer term yields would continue to decline. An ever-greater share of Lufthansa's revenues was generated outside of Germany, yet its cost base was still largely in the expensive *Standort Deutschland*. As further wage concessions could not be expected, Weber pinned his hopes on a new corporate structure of internal markets to create greater cost transparency, responsibility, and initiative in company operations. The idea was to split Lufthansa into several legally separate companies: Cargo, Technik (maintenance), and Systems (data processing) would all be separated from the mother company Lufthansa AG. The goal was to generate additional annual savings of DM 500–700 million by 1997. The Supervisory Board approved the restructuring in January 1994. Then, in September, it approved the business plans for three units becoming legally independent companies on January 1, 1995: Lufthansa Cargo AG, Lufthansa Technik AG, and Lufthansa Systems GmbH.

Lufthansa's approach can be characterized by the three concepts of *irreversible commitment*, *adaptive implementation*, and *overarching management guidance*. Lufthansa signaled irreversible commitment to internal markets by setting up its three new units as independent subsidiaries that by law must submit accurate balance sheets, profit-and-loss statements, and reports to shareholders. The Lufthansa group's adaptive implementation means corporate structures are in place that, as described later, guide the overall reform process as the new subsidiaries find their footing as market-facing units. Finally, the idea of overarching management guidance expresses Lufthansa's recognition that internal markets are not a panacea that will create all needed solutions in a vacuum; for internal markets to have their intended effect of fostering entrepreneurship and accountability at lower levels, the new corporate structure has to be complemented by strong leadership at the top of Lufthansa and by informal networking at lower levels.

To prepare for the January 1, 1995, deadline, a cross-unit project team began deliberations in April 1994 on how to structure relations between the business areas. In addition to the three new units just mentioned, Lufthansa had for a time investigated the feasibility of setting up yet two further units, Ground Service and Flight Operations, as subsidiaries or profit centers distinct from the Passenger Division. Furthermore, much of corporate overhead was compiled in a cost center for the corporate functions. To set up an internal market between all of these potential units required each area to establish, first, an inventory of the "products" it exchanged. An eight-by-eight matrix was set up to detail what the units would buy and sell to each other, as shown in Table 5.1.

The next step was to examine the interactions and decide on the pricing criteria to be applied and the degree to which transactions would be truly arms-length. Although the separation of Ground Service and Flight Operations ultimately appeared unfeasible for legal and technical reasons, the accounting systems for transactions between all other units were in place by early 1995. As one can imagine, the exercise of establishing accounting systems to handle transactions between so many different units was a major undertaking. The three new subsidiaries also had to work at breakneck speed to install systems enabling them to issue complete information for external and internal accounting purposes.

What did the new structure enable the new corporate units to do? First of all, it gave them greater freedom to grow their businesses by finding outside customers. All three new subsidiaries had achieved world-class competence in their areas.

Even prior to the new corporate structure Lufthansa was renowned for its maintenance operations; Technik AG did almost half of its work for outside customers right from the start. Lufthansa has been the world's largest cargo carrier since 1987, and thus the creation of Cargo AG was a natural step in its business development.

**Table 5.1. Input-Output Table of Lufthansa Units**

| Product Transfer From | Product Transfer To | | | | | | | |
|---|---|---|---|---|---|---|---|---|
| | Marketing | Operations | Maintenance | Flight Op's | Ground Op's | Cargo | Systems | Central Functions |
| Marketing | | 1 | 1 | 1 | 1 | 3 | 1 | 1 |
| Operations | 3 | | 1 | 1 | 1 | 2 | | 1 |
| Maintenance | | 3 | | 2 | 2 | | | |
| Flight Operations | | 3 | | | | 2 | | |
| Ground Operations | 3 | 2 | | 1 | | 2 | | 1 |
| Cargo | 1 | 1 | 2 | 1 | 1 | | | 1 |
| Systems | 3 | 1 | 2 | 1 | 3 | 2 | | 2 |
| Central Functions | 2 | 2 | 2 | 2 | 2 | 2 | 2 | |

Degree of interaction: 3 = high, 2 = medium, 1 = low

While leasing the bellies of the Passenger Division's aircraft on the internal market, Cargo AG acquired greater flexibility to build up its web of international alliances to provide global coverage at the lowest possible cost. Finally, changes in the global airline industry have made information processing systems as important a competitive tool as aircraft themselves, vital for computer reservation systems, cost accounting, flight scheduling, yield management, and frequent flyer programs. Upon updating its systems to leading-class levels, Lufthansa knew its expertise could be marketed on world markets. EDS, eager to gain a foothold in the lucrative aviation market, took a 25 percent stake in Lufthansa's new data-processing subsidiary, Lufthansa Systems. By expanding the business in the third-party market, System's ultimate goal was to reduce the in-house share of its revenue to 50 percent.

## Managing the New Corporate Structure

Sixteen thousand of Lufthansa AG's forty-four thousand employees were transferred to the new units at the beginning of 1995 (about ten thousand in Technik, five thousand in Cargo, and one thousand in Systems). Given the speed with which the new structure was implemented, Lufthansa had to design a system to monitor the functioning of the internal corporate market. The top-level guidance mechanism involved an ingenious change in the allocation of roles on Lufthansa's executive board, the *Vorstand*.

The *Vorstand* had traditionally comprised a chairman and five functional heads (of finance, personnel, maintenance, marketing, and operations) who decided policy on a collegial basis. Though remaining a collegial decision-making body, the *Vorstand* was henceforth composed of two distinct roles (see Figure 5.1). Three members (chairman, finance, and personnel) retained corporate-wide mandates, whereas the other two (marketing and operations) had functional responsibility for the activities of the Passenger Division. The idea was that while the Passenger Division would transact with the newly formed subsidiaries on a largely arms-length basis, the *Vorstand* would monitor the overall process to ensure that the unleashed corporate dynamics worked to the benefit of the Lufthansa group as a whole.

In other words, under the new corporate structure the mother company Deutsche Lufthansa AG was left with only the Passenger Division and the corporate functions: the formal *Vorstand* functions of finance and personnel continued to be headed by a *Vorstand* member; others (corporate controlling, strategy, and government relations) reported to the chairman. Thus, Lufthansa's highly innovative *Vorstand* structure looked as shown in Figure 5.1.

However, structure is only one part of the story. Lufthansa recognized that leadership and culture were equally indispensable to undergird the change process. In 1995 Weber intensified his worldwide series of town meetings in order to impress upon employees that Lufthansa's environment required cost reduction and adaptation to become a way of life. Weber emphasized that Lufthansa's internal markets were a valuable instrument in the struggle for greater flexibility and initiative, but the instrument could only work as well as the motivation of employees and the culture of the company allowed them to. As one marketing manager put it, "Many employees see Lufthansa making a decent profit in 1995, and think

**Figure 5.1. New Structure of Lufthansa Group**

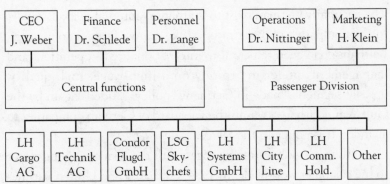

they can sit back and relax. That's why Weber is so keen to spread the message: 'People, that was only the beginning!' The turnaround and the new corporate structure are not one-time events, but part of a permanent effort. That's why *Überzeugungsarbeit* [the work of persuading people] is so important."

In addition to the need for overarching leadership, Lufthansa's new subsidiaries have recognized that exchange through internal markets needs to be supplemented by informal networking between units in many cases. For example, while passenger and cargo operations are now administered separately, many foreign countries prefer to deal with Lufthansa as a single entity and not as separate companies. Thus, internal markets paradoxically create the need for "soft" forms of cooperation such as networking and culture. Corporate leadership will become ever more critical, Lufthansa managers point out, as there are now more corporate units that are going their own way as indeed they were instructed to.

Within middle management, more responsibility has been delegated downward with more initiative being taken in many areas. The challenge for Lufthansa's management is therefore to encourage greater responsibility at lower levels in such a way that managers retain a view of the interests of the Lufthansa group as a whole.

## Going Global

The peculiarly German twist to Lufthansa's internal markets resides in the company's global strategy. Like many German companies, Lufthansa had been reluctant to internationalize its operations and management, preferring to rely on a high-wage, high-quality, upscale-segment "made in Germany" policy. "Aided" again by the Gulf War, Lufthansa was in the vanguard of German companies to abandon this policy in the 1990s.

Lufthansa's global strategy began with the goal of coming closer to the customer worldwide. In 1994, Lufthansa and United Airlines put together the world's first comprehensive global alliance of airlines with Thai Airways and a host of smaller carriers; SAS joined in 1995. The route networks, frequent flyer programs, and many other customer amenities were shared and a range of commercial activities more closely coordinated.

Yet there was a cost side to globalization as well, and this is where internal markets became so crucial to Lufthansa's competitiveness. Like other German companies, Lufthansa had to find ways to reduce the burden of its home country cost case, with its high wages, costly social benefits, and an ever-appreciating deutschmark. In 1995 Lufthansa repositioned itself in international competition with a wide-ranging program under the slogan "Going Global." Lufthansa's units and subsidiaries were invited to internationalize their operations further and thereby dilute the high cost of paying their expenses in deutschmarks. With the spin-off of Technik AG, Cargo AG, and Systems GmbH, these new companies acquired greater operational independence to step up their international activities, to forge links and acquire equity holdings in foreign countries, and to expand existing alliances. Weber stated quite openly, "Internationalizing our cost structure obviously means concentrating employee growth to a greater extent outside Germany—and not only because a global economy like Lufthansa needs a cosmopolitan workforce. Expanding our staff abroad also reduces costs and so safeguards jobs at home. The trade unions and staff councils are aware of this. We aim to pursue our strategy of 'Going Global' in concert with them."

Thus, Lufthansa Cargo AG set up a subsidiary in India and established secondary hubs in Sharjah and Bangkok. Lufthansa Technik AG shifted some of its work to its Irish joint venture, Shannon Aerospace. Indeed, Lufthansa AG itself moved some of its data-processing tasks to India and concluded an agreement with its unions in 1995 allowing it to hire up to 10 percent of its cabin crew in foreign countries at the lower prevailing wages. What internal markets allow Lufthansa to do is give different parts of the company both an incentive and the flexibility to adopt the globalization strategy that will best help them reduce costs. As Weber put it, "While Lufthansa generates only about half its income in deutschmarks, it has to pay for more than two-thirds of its expenditure in the strong German currency. We aim to lessen the risk stemming from this imbalance by shifting an appropriate portion of expenses out of the deutschmark and into softer currencies. That will make us less vulnerable to exchange rate fluctuations, which in 1995 alone cost the Company some DM 650 million in lost revenue."

Within this overall general deutschmark predicament that Lufthansa faces, the exchange rate disadvantage varies by unit. Systems GmbH started out selling most of its business to other units of the group, but Cargo AG received 99 percent of its revenue outside Lufthansa and about 75 percent outside Germany in 1995. Technik AG received about 40 percent of its revenue outside Germany and outside Lufthansa. For the Passenger Division of Lufthansa AG, about half the revenue is generated outside Germany. The "German" aspect of Lufthansa's internal markets, then, lies in allowing each company to adapt its global strategy to its own cost-revenue predicament. What "going global" implies in parallel to just solving the deutschmark problem, of course, is the human resource challenge of developing the Lufthansa "global manager." Yet this concept too is being implemented in different ways among the units.

Needless to say, this diversity of cost-revenue predicaments also led to major management challenges in internal pricing between Lufthansa units. In a globalizing company, what is the proper market price to apply? Are the prices charged to Technik AG's internal company customers to be based on comparable market prices within Germany? Within Europe? In the third world? These are difficult questions and were frequently raised. One of the principles that Lufthansa did try to apply in its first year of internal markets was to put a ceiling on the amount of energy devoted to arguments over pricing. As one top manager at Cargo AG put it:

If you have (say) fifty network managers from the Passenger Division and twenty from Cargo who busy themselves fine-tuning the transfer pricing between the units on every flight, there is a danger of our management capacities becoming focused on this task instead of the external market. How nice it is to argue with one's former colleagues! But whether the total transfer price is DM 10 million more or less really only concerns an internal corporate optimum. For me it's more important to position ourselves in the market: Where can I reduce costs, where can I earn more revenue? So the priority was to identify the most important economic factors, like the schedule, and then find a compromise.

## The First Year of Internal Markets in Practice

Having finished our overview of the rationale and framework for Lufthansa's internal markets, we asked how did the new units fare in their first year? To answer this question, let us examine the three cases separately.

### Technik AG

When the new corporate structure was being designed in 1994, many Lufthansa managers were concerned about whether the maintenance side of Lufthansa would be placed at a relative disadvantage if it had to transact on a market basis with the rest of the airline. Competition in the maintenance business intensified after the end of the Cold War as cuts in defense spending led to excess capacity in maintenance facilities for military aircraft; many of these facilities were then converted to civilian uses. To make matters worse, the major jet engine manufacturers have recently made increasing incursions into the maintenance field, thereby making the industry even more crowded.

Technik's willingness to take the plunge was based on great productivity strides it had made through process reengineering and on the courage of the division's designated head, who believed that lean management and aggressive pursuit of external business would allow the division to make profits. Under the new corporate structure the Passenger Division and Cargo wasted no time in demanding lower prices for maintenance services based on selected market comparisons. As foreseen from the beginning, these negotiations required the mediation of the three *Vorstand* members with corporate-wide responsibilities. The CEO and finance director had to ensure that actions taken by one part of Lufthansa to improve profitability did not reduce the profitability of the Lufthansa group as a whole. The personnel director had to ensure that industrial relations within the Lufthansa group remained intact.

In practice, mediation of discussions over transfer pricing and outsourcing for maintenance services involved the periodic arbitration of the corporate controller reporting to Weber. Corporate Controlling was summoned first to assess the appropriateness of the market price comparisons presented by Cargo and the Passenger Division. The second task of Corporate Controlling was to suggest remedies to the conflicts. This usually involved setting precise targets for cost and price reductions of given maintenance services over a specified number of years. As one Lufthansa manager put it, "A consequence of the new corporate structure is that the corporate controller is called upon to play a more sophisticated role than ever before."

## Cargo AG

The most important immediate consequence of the new corporate structure was the way it did business with the Passenger Division. In prior times, a fixed tonnage-mile cost was calculated on the bellies of passenger planes, irrespective of when the planes flew. The new internal market system created the need to assess the value of aircraft bellies on a flight-by-flight basis, taking into account the specific equipment, day of the week, and time of day of the flight. "Flights from Tokyo at noon provide almost no cargo value," explained Cargo's vice president for Controlling. "The lucrative business comes early in the morning or at the end of the business day."

The final outcome was very favorable to Cargo. The final lump sum paid by Cargo to the Passenger Division for aircraft bellies in 1995 was hundreds of millions of deutschmarks less than charged under the old system (the exact figures are confidential). In return, the Passenger Division was guaranteed a minimum level of cargo business for 1996.

In addition to this cost advantage, the interviewed Cargo managers stressed the emotional and political benefits of their newfound independence. Being "set free" reportedly liberated a lot of latent energy in the managerial ranks. It also created a platform to lobby for even more entrepreneurial freedom within the Lufthansa group. As one top Cargo manager put it, "On the revenue side we're in the Wild West. But on the cost side, many expenses are occasioned by Lufthansa. It's the very opposite of the Wild West. If you have your revenues in the Wild West, you must also be allowed to have your costs in the Wild West. Loosening these regulations on the cost side is an absolute precondition for the continued success of Cargo."

This manager happily acknowledged the benefits of belonging to the Lufthansa group and the value of the services rendered by Lufthansa AG's *Vorstand*-level functions: strategic coordination (chairman), financial and foreign exchange expertise (finance), and harmonized dealings with the unions (personnel). Even so, the Cargo *Vorstand* had a bone to chew: "Being truly a globally competing business, we would like to link managers' pay to performance beyond what is currently accepted practice in Lufthansa. It's a matter of ambition, really. When you play in the Wild West, you want to be paid in the Wild West."

### Systems GmbH

In its first year, 1995, Systems received 97 percent of its revenue from units within the Lufthansa group (Lufthansa AG, Technik AG, Cargo AG, and the charter and catering subsidiaries Condor and LSG). This figure would fall to 95 percent of its 1996 revenue of about DM 500 million, and by finding additional outside customers the in-house share of its revenue was supposed to fall to 50 percent. The Australian airline Ansett had signed up as Lufthansa's first major external airline customer for its network scheduling tools. The managing director of Lufthansa Systems reported in a 1996 interview:

> So far the new corporate structure has not been an excessive strain on us. We agreed with the *Vorstand* to reduce our unit prices on 80 percent of our business by 5 percent annually for the first three years. . . . We have drawn up finer-grained invoices for services than we used to, and there is greater transparency in costs and contracts. The new structure also has a psychological effect.  Outlays for data processing are now seen as real payments by our customers, whereas we increasingly have to justify the added value of what we do in relation to external suppliers.

## The Challenge Ahead

Under the new structure, Lufthansa's managers are more directly exposed to market realities in their particular operating domain. Two of these realities—high German exchange rates and intensifying competition in aviation—have promoted a common awareness among managers and employees that the company can only prosper on the basis of continual productivity improvement and innovation.

The spinning off of Cargo, Technik, and Systems is a critical step in diffusing the spirit of enterprise across the airline, but Lufthansa managers stress that it is only one step in the struggle to create a more dynamic, self-renewing organization. By bringing its managers into closer proximity to the laws of the marketplace, Lufthansa's reform has helped instill among company managers the understanding that the new corporate structure of internal markets is not just a one-time reform, but part of a dynamic process of change.

# Part II

# Forming a Network
# of Cooperative Alliances

# 6

# Knowledge Companies

## Gerald H. Taylor

I'd like to chisel out a different facet of this book's theme, and with the first cut I'd like to suggest a name for the new type of organization now emerging. Let's call them "knowledge companies." Knowledge companies compete not through size or industrial strength, but through the data they gather and distill about their markets and through the information technologies they use to reach customers in new ways.

Traditional corporate structure was a vertically integrated hierarchy arranged into functional departments to produce efficient operations. Knowledge companies, however, are decentralized aggregations of *multidisciplinary* teams or business units. They outsource nonstrategic functions to focus on their core competence, and are *virtually* integrated with other functional units and outside enterprises through alliances.

---

Gerald H. Taylor is CEO of MCI Communications Corporation, one of the fastest-growing telecommunications companies in the world. Over the past decade, MCI's share of the American market increased from 5 percent to 21 percent as the company introduced more than a hundred different service products, and its position in the Fortune 500 rose from 252nd to 66th.

Knowledge companies are needed today to manage the revolution in information technologies that is transforming economies. My favorite example is Mosaic Communications Company, whose breakthrough software Netscape first made browsing the Internet easy and that later became Netscape Corporation. With its enormous market power, you might expect this to be a well-established firm employing thousands of people. In 1996, Netscape celebrated its second anniversary with a total of 18 employees.

In today's competitive environment, corporate size means very little. By arming itself with information technologies, practically any size company can be a global player. What oil and steel represented to the industrial economy, innovation and knowledge represent to the information economy.

I would like to address four aspects of how MCI looks at this revolution: first, the revolution in information technology; second, the globalization of the marketplace; third, the growing—even voracious—demand for information and on-line services; and finally, the effects on business—how we're structured, how we compete, and how we manage.

## MCI's Forecast of the Information Revolution

Let's start with technology. Not long ago, it was commonly believed that computerization would lead to centralized control. Sophisticated papers were published in leading journals, such as the *Harvard Business Review*, predicting that corporations would be managed by large computers, and IBM estimated that the total market demand for computers throughout the world would amount to fifty-five machines. The attitude was best captured in the nagging fear that 1984 would really bring about George Orwell's vision of a Big-Brother type of society ruled by Big Computers.

But the reality turned out to be very different. History now regards 1984 not as a symbol of centralization, but as the beginning of the decentralization of information. In that year the Bell System was broken up, unleashing competition in telecommunications with a vengeance.

1984 was also the year when personal computers began to replace mainframes. *Time* magazine named the PC "Man of the Year" just a year earlier, Apple rolled out its first Macintosh, and Microsoft was putting the finishing touches on Windows 1.0.

In 1984, shipments of fiber optic cable in North America had grown from practically nothing to half a million kilometers annually, and an obscure military research network, later to be called the Internet, began to expand its presence.

In short, what we saw happening in 1984 was the Industrial Age being replaced by the Information Age. In 1991, for the first time ever, U.S. companies spent more on computing and information technologies than on any other form of investment. In the old days, the rule of thumb was that the power of a computer system increased by the square of its cost. According to the man who formulated this widely accepted law in the 1950s, Herbert Grosch, the bigger you go the more bang for the buck.

But Grosch could not foresee what the microprocessor would do to the computer world. The cost of computer processing, expressed in millions of instructions per second (MIPS), has fallen thousands of dollars in only a few short years. The cost of mainframe MIPS has fallen just as dramatically.

This exponential rate of performance improvement seems to defy the laws of physics; engineers are constantly finding ways to design ever-smaller circuits. In the 1970s, the standard "trench" forming the "wires" of a microcircuit was 6.5 microns wide—that's 6.5 millionths of a meter. On a chip the size of a thumbtack, you could cram about 2,300 transistors.

Today we're talking about trenches with a width of half a micron, even a tenth of a micron. In the not too distant future, one chip will be able to hold a billion transistors. Think about it: all the computing power that was utilized in NASA's Apollo program could fit in your wristwatch.

As this silicon real estate gets smaller and smaller, you get greater processing power, greater storage capacity, and greater capability for running complex applications. Here's what I mean. Ten years ago, mainframes could process twenty MIPS. Today, mainframes have moved up to four hundred MIPS, while workstations are capable of five. By the turn of the century, we're talking about mainframes performing at a hundred thousand MIPS, workstations at a thousand, and personal digital assistants—those little Newtons and Wizards you can hold in your hand—they'll run at five hundred MIPS. These small machines will have more computing power than practically any mainframe on the market today.

So let's summarize what these technology breakthroughs mean to our organizations. First, huge boosts in productivity. Computing technology is getting cheaper, more powerful, more plentiful, and more meaningful to business all the time.

Second, decentralized information systems that can respond more quickly in the marketplace. The mainframe was devoted to controlling information and centralizing decision making. The microprocessor has liberated users, empowered individuals, and decentralized access to information.

And third, innovation. As computing technology proliferates, the costs plummet and more companies go on-line, opening new markets and new opportunities.

## Globalization of Telecommunications

Of course, the Information Revolution is a global phenomenon. It's possible today to send a fax from Manhattan to Sri Lanka in a matter of seconds. You'll find cellular phones in the forests of Belize and satellite dishes on rooftops in Eastern Europe.

This sounds widespread, but the global telecom market is still in its infancy. There are nearly 6 billion people in the world, but only 643 million telephones. And that includes business phones. If you drew a map of the world based on the distribution of phone lines, you'd get a new kind of geography.

North America, Western Europe, and Japan account for nearly 75 percent of all existing phones in the world. Almost three-quarters of all telephones are located in countries with only 15 percent of the people. Consider that over half of the world's population has never made a phone call! Most people live more than two hours from a telephone. And fifty million people are on official waiting lists for phone service.

But the global market is growing up in a hurry. Some twenty-eight million phone lines were hooked up worldwide in 1992, thirty-three million more in 1993. Experts forecast that nearly a billion more people will have access to a telephone by 2000 A.D.

There are two implications of this global information environment. The first is an increasing trend toward globalization. Tip O'Neil said that all politics is local, but in commerce all business is global. Competition has moved from next door to anywhere in the world—business without borders. Why? Because information technology has liberated business from geographic and political boundaries. Money and ideas now move across these boundaries at the speed of light.

The second implication is that industries are converging. Where once there existed a sharp distinction between the telephone business, the computer business, and the entertainment business, now it's difficult to tell where each of these industries starts and another begins. In a market such as interactive multimedia, for instance, MCI's competitors are the long-distance companies, the telephone companies, and the cable companies, as well as Hollywood and Silicon Valley.

## The Voracious Demand for Information

Another phenomenon driving the creation of knowledge companies is the insatiable demand for information and on-line services. That story begins with the PC. The ubiquitous PC has become the networking terminal at the office and the on-line appliance in the home. Here's a key statistic. Twenty years ago, only fifty thousand computers existed in the entire world. Today, more than fifty thousand PCs are sold worldwide every ten hours. The number of computers in U.S. households has been doubling every five years. More than a third—or about thirty-five million households—now have computers.

Meanwhile, the installed base of PCs in U.S. business is nearly seventy-five million units. Business spending on computers and related services has doubled in the last decade, from around $80 billion in 1984 to nearly $160 billion today.

Actually, if you want to understand why the computer phenomenon is soaring, survey data tells the story. People today report that they spend almost as much time on their PC as they do on the telephone—eight hours and forty-eight minutes per week versus nine hours and thirty minutes.

The growth of on-line networks has also been an instrumental factor for knowledge companies. In 1979 there were just fifty-nine of these services in the United States. Today there are more than eight hundred. The latest figures from the Commerce Department show that almost 40 percent of all the PCs in the world are connected to networks. That's one reason why we expect business customers will be using more data than voice communications by the end of the decade.

From these trends, the shape of the information superhighway is clearly visible. In fact, it already exists in the Internet. The Internet may not be the ultimate network. But, like democracy, it's better than anything else available.

Back in 1984 the Internet was a tiny research network used by the military and the graduate assistants in college computer labs. Fewer than two hundred host computers were linked to it. Times sure have changed. According to a survey conducted in Spring 1997, the Internet is the number one topic of interest among business executives—higher even than NAFTA and health care. Stands to reason; the raw numbers on Internet usage are astounding. You've all read the stats: twenty to thirty million users, 3.2 million host computers, thirty thousand interconnecting networks with a new one added every thirty minutes.

What you may not realize is the Internet's tremendous potential for electronic commerce. As recently as five years ago the Internet and the corporate world were oceans apart. Mainframes dominated. Client-server networking was unheard of. And the only business conducted over the Internet involved federal research.

But today, commercial use accounts for more than half of all Internet traffic. That's one of the reasons why MCI and so many other companies are linking up to the Internet. You can have access to millions of customers both domestic and international. Products and services can be sold twenty-four hours a day. And because shipments are handled electronically, delivery costs are much lower. The former director of the Internet Society said the system can make any company a competitive player in the global arena if they know how to use its resources effectively.

This exploding demand for information around the world has caused an equally explosive rise in MCI's traffic. Ten years ago we had 3.5 million customers. Today, we have about twenty million, and in another ten years we expect to serve a hundred million people across the globe. Our billable calls grew from 1.8 billion to 22.7 billion in 1995, the equivalent of 5 calls for every person on the planet. In ten years we could carry almost three hundred billion calls per year. By then we'll probably be transmitting as much traffic in one minute as we do today in one year.

## Effects on Management

Relentless technological advances, globalization of commerce, and voracious market demand describe the external impact of this Information Revolution, but what about the internal impact? What impact are these issues having on the makeup and shape of the knowledge company?

We see several things happening. First, the traditional organization chart is being dismantled. Torn apart is more like it. Used to be if you wanted information you had to pry it out of the organization, and it was often filtered and politicized by middle managers. Most middle managers are really "human message switchers." They gather information, collate it, distort it a little, and hold on to it a lot, because information is power. Then, somewhere along the line, they distribute it. That message switching takes a long time, it's very expensive, and it stops the decision-making process cold.

Now, instead of message switching, you just tap in on electronic mail. Easy communication can exist across all levels in the organization. The old military-style chain of command is giving way to flatter, dynamic structures that make companies quick on their feet and more competitive in the marketplace.

Something else we see happening are fundamental changes in basic business processes. For instance, everything American business knows about marketing and distribution is up for grabs. As proof, dig out your company's marketing plan from just five years ago. I'd be very surprised if you don't find it incredibly out of synch with today's information economy. Today, suppliers and customers rummage around in each others' computers—entering orders, checking stock, verifying shipping. Salespeople routinely get instantaneous communication on orders and schedules.

*Fortune* magazine recently described how this part of the business has changed for a plastics manufacturer in Ohio. In the 1970s the company picked up its orders at the post office. In the early 1980s it put in an 800 number. In the late 1980s it added a fax machine. In 1991, it went to electronic data interchange. By 1993, more than half its orders arrived via modem straight into the company's computers. And the health of the company? Well, in twelve years sales have gone up eightfold.

Globalization and convergence make a couple of things clear. There is enormous pressure in this environment to produce innovative products and services, control costs, expand, and have greater speed to market. Also, no one company can do this all by itself. No company has all the needed access to capital, the resources, the talent, or the products and services to compete across all geographies and converging industry segments.

So competing globally means one thing: forging alliances and joint ventures. MCI, for instance, has forged more than a hundred alliances. We have marketing alliances with companies such as American Express and Northwest Airlines, technology alliances with companies such as Northern Telecom and Microsoft, and partnerships with British Telecom, NewsCorp, Microsoft, Banamex in Mexico, and Stentor in Canada.

By the way, I recently discovered the most definitive explanation of a joint venture. It comes from Mandarin Chinese. In that language, the literal translation of the phrase *joint venture* is "same bed, but different dreams."

Our goal in forging all these alliances is to create the first integrated communications company of the next century, one that can effectively provide a seamless web of all information services both locally and around the world. We are planning to spend $20 billion over the next few years to accomplish this guiding mission for MCI: we call it NetworkMCI. Half of all our revenue in the year 2000 should come from new products and services that we have yet to invent.⁴

With any alliance, the challenge is to make it work. Making sure the strategies and objectives are in synch can get rather complicated, as in our joint venture with British Telecom (BT). The most crucial requirement of a strong alliance is that each party bring something of value to the relationship. The combination of these contributions must also be greater than the value of either alone. In other words, the strength of an alliance is measured by the net economic value that it creates.

For instance, we bring MCI's well-known strengths of product development, marketing, and customized billing to our recent acquisition of Nationwide Cellular Services, which gives us access to

75 percent of the U.S. wireless communications market. This union of the unique assets of MCI and Nationwide is expected to make us "one of the wireless industry's most important distribution channels," as one analyst reported.

It is also crucial that both parties share a common sense of understanding and common view of the business world, and that they like each other as people. Our chairman, Bert Roberts, described his relationship with BT this way: "I don't think the BT-MCI deal could work if [BT chairman] Iain Vallance and I didn't have good rapport. We're not alike, but we get along well."

Our joint venture with BT has produced Concert, one of the world's most powerful international networks serving business needs. Now our corporate customers can combine voice and data services to integrate their operations around the world.

BT and MCI are also jointly providing first-class traffic on the Internet for private users who will pay a fee to get quick, reliable service. This venture, Concert InternetPlus, will increase the world's Internet capacity by 30 percent through fiber optic lines. Vint Cerf, our vice president for data architecture who was one of the original developers of the Internet, says this project "takes the Internet to its next major level of development to realize its well-accepted potential."

And our recent alliance with NewsCorp combines our networks with the enormous media content of the Murdoch empire. We expect this venture to provide people around the world with unlimited access to news, entertainment, and information services through the next generation of Internet systems.

We're also working on other alliances to provide local phone calls, direct broadcast television, and every other aspect of modern communication services. To achieve this ambitious goal, we realize we will have to master the art of modern management. With the blistering pace of change that's set by the information economy, just how does one get things done? It would be presumptuous of me to tell you that MCI has cornered the market on the management arts. But we have been in the thick of the Information Revolution; actually we're a *product* of it. Let me mention several things that have worked for us.

Point one: good management is a direct result of how well you know your business and your competitors. No surprise there. But there's a difference between knowing your business and *really* knowing your business. Really knowing your business requires using information technology. Not just for techies and accountants; managers must use information technologies and then lead by example.

Believe me, if top management uses information technology, everyone will follow suit. Bill McGowan, MCI's founder, used to call this "trickle-down high-tech."

Point two: when it comes to information technology, focus on the information and let others worry about the technology. You don't need to understand the nuances of computers and networking any more than driving a car requires understanding how to rebuild a carburetor.

Point three: embrace change. Most companies go to great lengths to avoid any kind of change. For them, change is like a snakebite— one hit and they're paralyzed. For MCI, change has always meant new opportunities. We're not only used to change in the telecommunications business, we invent a lot of it ourselves.

One of the ways we do that is by regularly moving people in our organization to new assignments and new work teams. And when it comes to hiring, a key philosophy at MCI is, "Preserve the MCI culture but don't hire in your own image." We've always believed that when people in the organization look differently, think differently, and act differently, the business will stay fresh and innovative.

Point four: use the Net. We tell our leaders that good decision making is directly proportional to the amount of information they put into their heads. The more information they cram in, the better their decisions. There's a wealth of information available today— through the Internet, on-line services, CDs, you name it. By taking advantage of what's out there, we see our opportunities more clearly and can speed up our reaction time.

Point five: keep an eye on small entrepreneurs and progressive companies. That's where new ideas come from. Ideas, in our business, are worth their weight in gold; they're an essential raw material. After all, the company most likely to do us damage isn't a current competitor but one outside our industry—a company armed with a new technology or idea that will bring about profound change. Typewriters weren't done in by other typewriters, but by word processors and PCs. Tin can manufacturers are getting hit by the makers of those drink boxes that come with a straw attached, which only your kids understand how to use. The message is clear: if we spend time watching just our obvious competitors, sooner or later we'll be surprised.

Point six: treat technology as a slave and treat people as royalty. MCI has been thought of as a high-tech company. But it's not technology that differentiates MCI, nor financial strength, nor just marketing skill. What differentiates MCI is its people and its organization. Most companies have spans of control and layers of management. MCI people have built spans of *teamwork* and layers of *leadership*.

## The Challenge of a New Economic Paradigm

My intention in this chapter is to give you some sense about how MCI is reading the Information Revolution, and how that revolution is creating what we call "knowledge companies." But I've learned that predicting the future based on the present is dangerous.

After all, history is full of cautionary examples. Alexander Graham Bell believed the telephone would be used to broadcast music to people in remote areas. The radio was invented with the idea of replacing telephones. Television was intended to be a visual medium that offered two-way communication.

At MCI, we believe the future is not a question of whether we will have new and more powerful information technologies. We will. However, the future is not about some interesting new services for our customers. And it won't be driven by trivial applications such as having more movies on demand.

Rather, the future is about a new paradigm: the building of an infrastructure for a new and quite different economy where the building blocks are innovation and knowledge. What it comes down to is this: in the old industrial economy, a business gained market power by controlling information; in the new information economy, a business gains market power by providing greater access to the information.

All of our organizations will be transforming to keep up with this new information economy. No doubt about it, it's going to be like a roller coaster. We'll be surprised—and we'll be thrilled by the incredible new business opportunities it will bring. And I can tell you, MCI is looking forward to the ride.

# 7

# The Spherical Network Organization

## Raymond E. Miles

The technological revolution is the driving force behind organizational change today. It's not only the rapid pace of technological advances, but the way technology, new ideas, and knowledge are racing around the world at the speed of light. That's why organizational change is moving at a rate beyond anything in our recent memory.

I was vividly impressed on that point recently in South America when speaking to a group of about a thousand managers. At the first break, the entire audience stood up, everyone reached in their briefcase, pulled out a cellular phone, and started dialing. I had this impression that they were all calling one another. Out in the lobby, I noticed vending machines dispersing cellular phones for rental.

---

Raymond E. Miles is Trefethen Professor of Organizational Behavior Emeritus at the Haas School of Business, University of California, Berkeley. He served as dean of the school from 1983 to 1990, and he was also director of the Institute for Industrial Relations. Miles has authored numerous articles and books; his most recent book, coauthored with Charles Snow, is *Fit, Failure, and the Hall of Fame* (New York: Free Press, 1994).

## The Evolution of New Organizational Forms

These powerful forces of technological innovation are the main reason why our organizations have become unglued. In many industries today, the innovation cycle is now shorter than the planning cycle that managers use to introduce new products. Their customers are actually moving faster than the company's ability to manage. If that is the case, well, you are behind the learning curve. Not a very useful place to be.

However, we know what we must do to respond. We must invent new strategies, new structures, and new ways of managing. We know that because we have faced this problem in the past. If you look back over the last 150 years or so, we can see several periods of major change.

At the turn of this century we faced a rapid expansion in domestic markets, which required large, vertically integrated organizations that could accomplish economies of scale to deliver goods efficiently. Carnegie, Ford, and other great entrepreneurs led in the creation of these vertically integrated, functional hierarchies. Many firms emulated those pioneers. Others did not get the package right and failed.

As domestic markets matured in the 1920s through 1950s, diversification became the new strategy. General Motors, Wards, and Sears taught us how to form decentralized, multidivision organizations that focused on diverse markets. This was a sharp break from the past. Again, many firms copied the leaders. Some got it right. Some did not. Many failed. Often firms tried but did not accomplish true decentralization. They suffered all of the costs of decentralization but gained none of the benefits because corporate management never learned to relinquish control.

In the 1950s and 1960s, far more complex mature markets pushed us to develop equally complex mixed structures and matrix organizations. Throughout this period there was a common prescription, even though we changed organizational forms several times. That prescription was to get better by getting bigger. As each new opportunity emerged, we simply pulled more things under the same organizational umbrella and managed to achieve better coordination and synergy. This trend toward getting bigger, however, seems to have run its course and has now ended.

The reversal of this decades-long trend can be seen in today's downsizing, outsourcing, and other new practices. In other words, we are at the beginning of another new organizational form. Instead of getting bigger and searching for greater internal synergy, the new prescription is to focus on an organization's distinctive strengths. Firms are increasingly searching for those arenas in which they can add greater value than their competitors. The new prescription is to downsize to one's assets and core competencies that can be best employed.

As pressure mounts to be more efficient and highly responsive, we simply cannot tolerate the higher costs and complexity that was normal just a decade or so ago. Before, a firm might well have held a factory that was only utilized thirty or forty hours a week. Today, we probably cannot tolerate this underutilization of capital, equipment, or people. We used to stockpile people for possible use; now we have to use all their capabilities fully.

For some organizations the search for additional efficiency and flexibility will lead them all the way to network organizations that create value by using information to innovate continually—a totally new form.

## Types of Network Organizations

There are probably at least three common network types. The easiest to imagine is the stable network. This form takes us the shortest distance away from what we are familiar with. Organizations simply shrink their value-added processes and outsource upstream to suppliers and downstream to distributors. Nike is a good example of a stable network. The great advantage of this form is that the company is relatively small considering its total volume of activity. Nike has a small set of assets under its direct control, yet it has a large stable network of global suppliers and a large stable network of global distributors. Nike manages this network but directly controls only a small part of it.

A more exotic network form is what we have called a dynamic network. The dynamic network differs from a stable network in the rapidity with which it changes partners. A broader network of potential partners gives a firm additional access to capabilities and additional flexibility. The publishing industry frequently operates exactly in this fashion—relatively small assets under the control of the publisher, but an incredibly large network of printers, graphic artists, copy editors, and so on. The movie industry in recent years has operated with a global network of studios and sound editors. And the fashion world is frequently a dynamic network also.

The dynamic network itself is now evolving into a still more sophisticated system that draws on the special knowledge available throughout its network of partners to form a unique capability for continual, specialized innovation. It solves problems, creates new goods and services, and designs entirely new applications—and it does so efficiently. Advertising agencies and design firms are good examples. They treat each client as an individual project requiring an original solution. You never see the same commercial for two different products.

We are also seeing an increasing array of internal networks. In this model, firms may continue to own major assets, but instead of using central planning mechanisms to guide their internal operations they use market mechanisms.

Perhaps the most fully developed example is Asea Brown Boveri (ABB), the Swedish producer of electrical equipment and contracting services. ABB operates globally using three different types of business units all owned by the parent company: local companies that serve a domestic market in some nation, research and manufacturing plants that produce goods for use throughout the ABB system, and a trading company that coordinates across these two types of organizations. These units collectively form over a thousand profit centers, all interacting with one another. Management's task in this instance is no longer managing assets, but managing the market within which assets are allocated.

As managers move from the traditional organizational form to a network, a wide range of issues arise and new problems emerge. This can be best illustrated by focusing for a moment on what we are dealing with as we think about the network organization. We are dealing with three different components: *of a network system.*

1. The central or host firm that forms the "core" of the network because it usually plays a dominant role as the designer of the product

2. The set of other organizations—usually suppliers, distributors, and customers—that fill out and connect the network in action at any given time

3. The population of organizations from which they may draw their next set of partners

For example, Ford is forming a network as it continues to outsource, reducing its control over the total value-added in its cars from 65 percent down to 38–39 percent today. Dell Computer is the core of a network because it designs and distributes PCs but manages a worldwide array of components producers. And there is the famous Wintel network composed of thousands of computer parts manufacturers, software designers, and other firms that have gravitated around the Microsoft operating systems and Intel chips that form the heart of most PCs.

Note that all of these actors are organizations in their own right. This means that participating in a network requires learning how to manage interorganizational relationships in a complex flow running from raw materials to distribution. Tasks that used to be internal—for example, team building—now become interorganizational. Managers have to learn to build teams across organizations that are partnering. They have to manage an effort to pull together a customer, distributor, supplier, and designer into a working partnership that may last only for one major delivery of a product or service. This means learning to collaborate across organizations.

But network structures also demand that we go beyond just recognizing how to put networks together and managing complex interorganizational relationships. We also have to focus on managing each organization in the network using a far more flexible, adaptive approach. We are at the stage now where we are beginning to recognize that a network firm will be only as effective in a network as it is internally.

To achieve this internal effectiveness in a network we probably need two things. We need a new metaphor—a new way of thinking about the organization—and a new management philosophy. Let me suggest possible solutions to these needs that appeal to me based on observations of the most advanced network organizations.

## The Spherical Metaphor of a Network Organization

The network firm is clearly going to move from a hierarchical model of organization to something more dynamic. I want to suggest that we think of the network organization as being spherical. A spherical organization can rapidly rotate its resources to meet the needs of upstream and downstream partners. If a company is organized hierarchically—as a pyramid—it can only have one or two points that an upstream or downstream partner can plug into.

The most advanced network organizations look very different from this pyramid metaphor—they behave as though they were spherical systems. I can approach them at any point, and when I establish contact with a network organization, the resources needed for my connection rotate to meet my needs. Here's a good example. Nordstrom, the department store chain, is so dedicated to high service that any door you enter opens up the whole system and orients itself to serving your special needs. Another is an Australian firm, which I will say more about later, that is able to rotate all its resources to meet global needs at any given moment. Although it is a very small firm, it behaves as though it is an enormous global enterprise simply because every piece of its internal machinery is completely flexible and rotatable.

If organizations can achieve this level of dynamism, infinitely connectable upstream and downstream, then they become far more effective network members. Of course, not every organization is going to achieve this level of sophistication.

## The Human Investment Philosophy

To achieve this high degree of flexibility, network companies also have to make substantial investments in their people. We toss terms like "empowerment" around casually. But we badly need not only a new metaphor of organization, we also need a new philosophy of employee relations. The most advanced firms are achieving spherical capabilities through a very simple mechanism: heavy investment in their employees.

Empowerment occurs when work teams move past the immediate technical needs of their organization through training and education and step ahead to gain an understanding of the entire business. A good team should be capable of meeting with a security analyst to discuss the factors affecting the company's stock price and its cost of capital. Members should understand innovations underway in other firms and industries. Every member of every team has to know precisely how the organization makes money and how it is governed. They need to possess advanced knowledge of self-management practices and an awareness of the management systems operating up and down the network chain.

That does not come automatically and it does not come easily. It will only come when organizations spend the money necessary to produce fully competent people. There is emerging now in the most advanced organizations a new human resources prospective. These organizations invest heavily in continual education for their permanent workforce. Rather than exploiting the workforce by bringing in the cheapest temps, they use professional temporary workers. They also contract only with agencies that are themselves investing and constantly upgrading their temporary workers. They focus on growth and employability for both their permanent and temporary workers.

The job may be disappearing, but the career is not. What we have to begin to offer people is not necessarily a stable job, but highly developed career prospects—employability. Employees may only stay in an organization for a few years as the economic demand for their skills shifts, but they should be constantly advancing in their knowledge and skills. If we can offer people that through continuing education and training, jobs will still be there but in the form of dynamic careers.

In the most advanced organizations we are seeing the emergence of a "human investment philosophy." This philosophy holds that the way to the future is through investment in human resources. At the turn of the century, managers changed philosophies from Social Darwinism to human relations. We learned how to treat people nicely enough so they would remain as part of a stable workforce. Henry Ford advanced this concept by giving his workers five dollars a day and a pat on the back. He understood that you have to pay people enough to buy your product and that you have to keep them on the job to operate a mass production system.

As the 1950s and 1960s turned to the decentralized matrix organization, we learned to go beyond that with a human resources perspective that focused on utilizing people more effectively. We moved from job enlargement to job enrichment. Today we must move beyond that to empowerment. And the only way to empowerment is through heavy investment. The human investment model states that people can advance far beyond their present capabilities if we can invest heavily in education and training to develop more sophisticated skills.

But I want to emphasize that this is an *investment* philosophy, because we are not simply paying for skills that are already visibly needed. That is not investment. Investment requires taking a risk. Investment is in education and training that goes beyond our present needs to anticipate the needs of an uncertain future. There is risk involved, certainly, but the risk is warranted because of the great need to develop important new reservoirs of capability.

This human investment philosophy is highly visible across the country. At the individual level, for example, firms such as Chaparral Steel are investing as much as a third of everyone's time every year in education. They are taking people well beyond their presently known business needs simply to produce know-how capacity to meet a future requirement. Southwest Airlines is investing heavily in cross-training to give its employees a continuing edge in rapid-turnaround operations; everyone understands everyone else's job because that is their method of staying ahead of their competitors. Semco, the Brazilian firm, is investing in education that has allowed some of its low-level employees to spin off their own business firms to become suppliers. Motorola, Nike, and Novell all are fine examples of firms that are taking this human investment model across entire organizations; they are prepared to invest not only in their own firm but in other firms working with them in their network. Bringing one's partners up to your level of knowledge is a way of enhancing your own capability.

## Future Developments

I would like to close this analysis of network organizations by telling you about a very unusual company that has integrated all these points powerfully.

Technical Computer Graphics is a relatively small company in Australia with probably no more than 250 employees. It is made up of a number of small "cellular" firms who have banded together in continuing alliances. The most advanced networks today are composed of such cellular units: collections of self-managing teams, or cells, that are each good at problem solving and forming alliances with other teams inside or outside the corporation. We call these units cells because, like the pieces of a living organism, they share the same essential characteristics of the larger organism, and they grow, learn, and evolve together.

Each of these cellular firms brings complementary technological competencies to the network. They constantly operate as entrepreneurs, seeking out new ventures globally. As they come up with an idea believed to be valuable, they search immediately for a potential customer; that key customer in turn becomes a partner in the development of the product. They also look for external suppliers who may bring additional technical capabilities to the venture, and they look internally to find other members of the TCG family with whom they can partner.

Thus, a triangle of principle customers, joint venture partners, and TCG network companies emerges. It is a rich technological package put together for the delivery of a particular product or service. Each such project is viewed as an opportunity to tap the problem-solving expertise of its network partners and to ensure that the knowledge learned from this experience is widely shared within the corporation. Thus, in networks composed of cellular units, the collective experience of the cells and the management of this knowledge become the crucial elements for success.

Furthermore, in each of these cellular firms every individual is expected to be a supporting member of the team. For another venture, any of these same individuals may be the leader in an entrepreneurial effort. These teams are completely rotatable and constantly interactive.

TCG also makes a continuing investment in helping each member develop a complete knowledge of what is occurring throughout the system. Virtually everyone across the organization is fully aware of the total set of activities going on in TCG at any given moment. They may not be fully competent to do each one, but they are able to guide an internal or external resource to the proper connection inside the network.

This looks to me like the future—not the future for every firm, but for many firms. This will only occur to the extent that we get a very clear notion of the operational logic of the network organizational form. We must also develop a philosophy of management that allows us to see empowerment as a necessity, and to base empowerment on continuing investment in human resources.

We're still a long way from knowing as much as we need to  about designing organizations that create and use knowledge, that are good at continual learning, and that can innovate specialized solutions to suit unique needs. We know it depends on widely shared interactive communication. We also know it is stimulated by collegial behavior and shared respect. Cellular structures made up of small face-to-face units tied together by norms of respect and sharing seem to be increasingly common in the most productive knowledge industries. But we have to learn much more about how to create and encourage such environments.

We are not likely to reach this future by applying traditional management philosophies, even if we do so with a new organizational form. The whole package has to be in place.

# 8

_What applies to one level applies to another in terms of teamnets_

# The Age of the Network

## Jessica Lipnack and Jeffrey Stamps

In 1993, Pennsylvania's Erie County Economic Development Council named Harry Brown "Employer of the Year." Brown is one of the most successful "teamnet" (a network of teams) executives in the United States, though his company may not fit your image of the exemplary twenty-first-century organization.

First, he's not in an information industry. His corporation, EBC Industries, Inc., formerly Erie Bolt Company, literally makes nuts and bolts. Second, instead of trying to stamp out or buy out his competitors, he regularly partners with them. And finally, he mentors them. They remain independent and so does he.

"I've figured it out," Brown says. "I woke up at four o'clock this morning and finally figured out why we're different. Most companies focus on the competition, how to beat the competition. We focus on the customer, how to meet the customer's needs."

---

Jessica Lipnack and Jeffrey Stamps are a wife-and-husband team who helped pioneer the study and practice of organizational networks. They cofounded The Networking Institute in 1982 and have published five books, the most recent being _Virtual Teams_ (New York: Wiley, 1997). This chapter is adapted from their book _The Age of the Network: Organizing Principles for the 21st Century_ (New York: Wiley, 1996. © 1996 John Wiley & Sons. Reprinted by permission.)

This simple shift enables Brown to take off the typical business blinders. With his enthusiasm and energy, he has transformed a failing Rust Belt business—forty-six employees, barely $3 million in revenues, losing at least $100,000 a year and about six months from bankruptcy—into a thriving enterprise with a hundred employees and revenues of $8 million. Note also that he started this turnaround just before the 1987 stock market crash, when the U.S. economy fell into recession.

Brown and his cadre of cooperating competitors are hard-working and very successful at what they do because they have the following:

- A common business purpose: profit that comes from serving customer needs

- Twenty or so allies, each with an independent specialty

- Intense communication across and within company lines—meetings, faxes, phone calls, visits

- Lots of leaders, with leadership shifting depending on the task at hand

- Participation at all levels of all companies, each of which is a part of many wholes

"I started doing this because it was common sense," Brown says simply. "If times weren't tough, I probably wouldn't have thought of it. But when things aren't going well, you're willing to try anything."

It all began when a customer asked Brown for something he didn't have. "A customer's order required secondary machining operations that we didn't have in-house," Brown explains. "So I called up a competitor, Joe Fedorko at Diversified Manufacturing Company, who did, and it worked."

It worked so well that the next time Brown got an order he couldn't fill, he approached another competitor to whom he'd once subcontracted. "We found that they enjoyed doing business with us because there were no surprises. We shared process information, which reduced the number of rejects and streamlined production flow," says Brown. "This grew our product base, and we all started growing together."

Indeed, today Brown's idea is a thriving network that operates as a virtual factory complex—including competing specialty plating and coating companies, heat-treaters, and machine shops.

There is nothing all that arcane about it. "When we get a blueprint, we get together to discuss the best way to meet those requirements," Brown explains. "As soon as we arrive at the proper manufacturing process, we discuss costs to make sure we're competitive. Then we submit the bid."

They realize a 30 percent cost saving by fully using each others' capabilities, an advantage they pass on to customers with lower prices and to themselves in reduced manufacturing expenses. Remarkably, each company has more than doubled its business.

There are challenges, however, to regarding one another as virtual extensions of each other. It means they share manufacturing process information, something most competitors fear. "There's always the potential that one of the companies might try to take on the business themselves," Brown says. "This happened once, but in the end they lost the business because they didn't have the strength of the network. Word spread pretty rapidly and it was difficult for them to create the relationships they needed to fulfill the contract. Violation of trust never works."

People from all the companies also walk in and out of each others' shops, a practice virtually unheard of in the highly competitive manufacturing world. They can spot new business opportunities and improve their processes as the firms learn about one another's operations.

For example, Brown's company could produce a computer numerically controlled (CNC) machine part. "One of the companies in the network did not have the CNC software they needed to do the process efficiently," Brown recalls. "So we gave them our program, they modified it to fit their machine, and they did the operation more efficiently."

Although they sometimes compete for the same business, they think the gains of sharing information far outweigh the risks of revealing trade secrets, Brown says.

Even the unions are on board. EBC Industries was the first company in the United Steel Workers to sign a five-year contract, which includes provisions for flexible work schedules, in-house technical training, cross-training on three pieces of equipment, and profit sharing. "Pay levels increase as people gain additional technical expertise," Brown reports.

In 1990, EBC received the Pennsylvania Governor's Labor-Management Cooperation Award. "The union doesn't have any problem with this approach," says Brown. "They see that while there are layoffs all over town in union shops, we're hiring. Management and labor are working together to make sure jobs are more permanent than they were in the past."

It's a rather impressive story taken as a whole—a nuts-and-bolts company cooperating with its competitors and getting along with the union. EBC Industries' network shares five key principles with other teamnet organizations.

## Five Teamnet Principles

You don't have to change everything to move into the Age of the Network. Harry Brown has created a teamnet with his competitors that offers their Industrial Age product in an Information Age style of business. Brown successfully and aggressively engages in *coopetition*: he cooperates with his competitors for business that he cannot do alone.

Let's look closely at the EBC strategy and note its five distinguishing features:

1. *Unifying Purpose*. Shared commitment to the same goal, not legalisms, holds the firms together.

When asked the purpose of his network, Brown simply says "profit." He also talks constantly about delighting his customers. He knows why he formed the network. Initially, it was for survival; then, it proved to be very good for business.

2. *Independent Members*. Each company is different. Each retains its independence while it cooperates with others on specific projects.

Brown quickly reels off nine firms when asked to name the companies in his network, from the 5-person contract machine shop, D&E Manufacturing, to the 130-person Erie Plating Company, which does special plating that meets very stringent government specifications. Later that day, he faxed us a list of twelve additional companies, with names like American Tinning and Galvanizing, Hytech Metals, and Machining Concepts. There is no formal, set-in-stone membership—including about a dozen firms involved from the early days—and each is completely independent of, though also interdependent with, the others.

3. *Voluntary Links*. They communicate extensively and meet often. No one is forced to participate. There are many criss-crossing relationships.

"There are no regular meetings. No one wants them except on an as-needed basis to address problems as they surface," Brown says. "Then we involve whoever's working on the project. We meet right on the shop floor. We have dry chalk boards by the machines so people can make notes as they go along. People know each other well. We fax a lot. We've experimented with e-mail but mostly what we look at is graphics so fax is easier. Social get-togethers just happen—nothing formal."

Almost as afterthought, he says, "We had some golf outings."

4. *Multiple Leaders*. Different people and companies lead depending on what needs doing. During any given process, more than one person leads.

"It's not so much product driven as process driven, so this happens automatically," Brown explains. "On one project, Champion Bolt [an Erie distributor and small-scale manufacturer of fasteners] had the initial lead in specifying the parts.

"Then, we were working on some very difficult stainless steel material. We don't know that technology, so a vendor in our manufacturing group, Ron Wasielewski, who is a technical specialist in the latest cutting tools at Erie Industrial Supply, led that discussion. Now we're all at a higher level of knowledge."

Next, Russ Mollo, Brown's chief engineer, jumped back in when it came to heat treating. So it goes, with leaders changing over time.

"Russ is our resident agent of change and constant reminder to pull in all available resources to advance technologically and personally," Brown says. "Traditional job functions are gradually disappearing. As time goes on, there will be no defined engineering department, no defined sales department. The new organization will be a blend of various functions resulting in streamlined communications and a more responsive source for our customers."

5. *Integrated Levels*. People work at many levels within EBC and other partner companies in the teamnet. This network itself is part of the nuts-and-bolts business, which is embedded in the Erie County economy, which contributes to the U.S. industrial base.

The owners of the firms, the hierarchy, are not the only ones who work together; the "lower-archy" does too. "Machine operators talk directly to one another. It may be rare in other shops but it's common practice here," Brown says. Communication is direct and doesn't have to go through approved channels.

Brown hesitates for a moment when asked to name the departments within his own company. "Well, let's see. The departments kind of blend into each other." He mentions marketing and sales first, describing Vice President Norm Strandwitz as a "great advocate of team play and information sharing so that more information surfaces. He spends a lot of time on the shop floor."

Then Brown stops to think again, and says, "When you get past marketing, right around that same level, I'd put our QC [quality control] manager, Dan Neal." Brown goes on to describe the rest of the organization, including Joe Legnasky, the purchasing manager; Lew Vespoli, the treasurer, who "gets out on the shop floor"; Bob Valimont, the manufacturing manager, "who puts up with people strolling in and out of the shop"; right down to "the foreman in the forge shop and the hourly workforce with group leaders."

Obviously Brown isn't an executive who spends his days carefully designing and studying his organization chart. He just lives it. Brown also sets his shop in a larger context, beginning with the Greater Erie area. "Any Rust Belt community has to look at what's happened to their business in the past and change," he says. "Then we are part of the nation's manufacturing base to compete globally. We have to pool our management skills so we can learn about our technology needs and assist one another."

## A Pocket Tool for Teamnets

Consider the five teamnet principles together as a mental tool, a Swiss Army pocketknife of the mind. Each principle is a separate tool that you can pull out and apply to your situation. They address different aspects of networks, but together they capture the integrated elements of a whole. "Doing it right" means that you have used each principle appropriately, in the proper measure. When you succeed, you have a healthy teamnet. Following is an elaboration of—and a few warnings about—each principle.

1. *The Purpose of Purpose:* Purpose is the glue and the driver.

Every teamnet needs a clear purpose: "Win the new jumbo jet systems integration contract and prepare our company to deliver it," says the computer company bid team. "Implement the new schedule planning process by 1 June," says the airline. "Cut operating costs by 20 percent in sixty days," says the hotel chain.

Teamnets achieve success by clearly defining their purpose. It needs to be simple and everyone involved needs to understand it and, if possible, participate in its development. Each project in Harry Brown's manufacturing network has its clear purpose that derives from its overall one of meeting customer needs and making a profit.

Purpose must extend from the abstract to the concrete to be truly useful. It begins with the organization's long-term vision, values, and strategy. These abstractions must translate into time-bound operational missions, measurable goals, clearly identifiable results, and, finally, specific tasks. Action must accompany beliefs and commitments, or the circuit never closes.

Purpose plays an absolutely critical role in teamnets. It establishes legitimacy, functioning in the place of the hire-fire power of hierarchy and the rules and regulations of bureaucracy. It is the basis for the agreements and voluntary relationships that constitute the "work life" of the network.

Which is not to say that purpose isn't important to other forms of organization. "What you're talking about are the Nine Principles of War," said Karl Leatham, a retired Army lieutenant colonel and now a business process reengineering expert at Computer Sciences Corporation. "Just substitute the word 'competition' for 'enemy' and 'purpose' for 'target,' and you'll see what I mean."

Failure is easier to predict than success. A range with extremes can express each of the principles. We portray these extremes as "warnings" because they function as failure detectors. So problems with purpose can range from too little to too much. Keep in mind that each is not the opposite but the complement of the other extreme. When one tendency threatens the health of a network, you then need to introduce a dose of the other.

*Warnings: From Glueless to Groupthink.* Networks fail without enough purpose—enough being an imprecise quantity that always depends on local circumstances and timing. Mostly, people know a motivating purpose when they both can feel its power and understand its compelling logic. Teamnets, however, easily can fall apart after they form when the spark of purposeful life flickers and dies. Purpose is a vital source of energy that needs regular renewal, more often the more things change.

The more obscure extreme and source of failure is too much purpose. "Groupthink" can also kill a network. People can lose their critical faculties when they are so cohesive that they become cult-like. Purpose turns into ideology as the group discourages critical thinking. People make expensive mistakes when they put blinders on and refuse to tolerate divergent ideas. The need for diversity around purpose underlies the importance of independent members.

2. *Declaration of Independence:* Each member has a healthy independence.

Think of it as a key test: you are not in a network if joining means you have to give up your independence. Members of networks—individuals in self-directed teams, departments cooperating in cross-functional programs, firms in alliance—retain and usually enhance their independence.

The parts of traditional organizations are dependent on a central and higher authority. Each company in Harry Brown's network stands on its own footing. Each will continue to exist even if the network collapses.

This principle underlies VISA International. Financial institutions totaling twenty-three thousand companies create its products accepted by eleven million merchants in 250 countries and territories whose data centers clear more transactions in one week that the Federal Reserve system does in a year. Sales now equal the combined revenues of General Motors and IBM, having grown 20–50 percent compounded annually since VISA's birth in 1970. Dee Hock, founder and CEO emeritus of VISA International and VISA USA, established the business on simple principles, many of which stress the independence of the members:

- Equitable ownership by all participants

- Maximum distribution of power and function

- Distributed authority within each governing entity; and,

- Infinitely malleable yet extremely durable.[1]

Consider, by analogy, the epochal change in the nature of computing in the last decade. Engineers designed computer systems in "master-slave" arrangements for most of the first 40 years: a glass-enclosed host computer with "dumb" dependent terminals attached. The entire system crashed when the central unit went down.

The unquestioned hegemony of huge machines in the Information Age was first cracked by the computer on a chip in the mid-1970s, which led to the PCs that decimated the centralized behemoths. The architecture of networks is ascendant in computing in the 1990s. PCs, workstations, mainframes, and other intelligent devices represent the independence of members connected in networks.

Members of a network are so substantial in their self-sufficiency that they do not depend on the network itself. A healthy independence is necessary, even a prerequisite, for healthy interdependence.

*Warnings: From Dependent to Stubborn.* Networks fail at one extreme when their participants, whether organizations or individuals, cannot behave independently. This is the source of many network failures in large bureaucratic cultures. Bureaucrats may be free in theory but in practice they fear making decisions and prevent others from taking responsibility that constitutes real independence. If you want a more flexible organization, be prepared not only to tolerate but vigorously support risk taking.

People also carry independence to the other extreme: to stubbornness, where their narrow-minded behavior overwhelms cooperative efforts. Those who are so independent that they can't see a common purpose fragment the network, destroy its coherence, and doom it to fail. Small business networks often fail because some members just are too stubbornly independent.

3. *Link City, Planet Earth:* Teamnets have many links—expansive relationships among people and extensive connections through technology.

Many people wrongly regard a network as nothing more than a mesh of physical links. Even so, they unconsciously point to the network's distinguishing feature. Links—multifaceted, omnidirectional, complex, technical, and personal—are the cardinal characteristic of the Information Age organization.

Look first to see your links in the physical communication systems besides meetings and collocation that you use (or soon will): phones, faxes, memos, letters, overnight mail, conferencing (phone, video, computer), e-mail, the Internet, cellular phones, mobile computing. The list goes on, and these are only the person-to-person media.

It's not news that our world is more connected than ever and that the trend still is accelerating. It's a blind spot, though, when people think that networks only mean computers, telephones, and other channels of communication.

Even technology networks are more than computers and telephones. What use is an e-mail or voice mail system if people aren't using it? Cayman Systems, a network hardware vendor, advertises that it "hasn't forgotten that what we're really connecting is people, not just computers."

People develop relationships over time through their interactions. They must use some physical links to communicate—channels to interactions to relationships and back.

Technology alone is inert. Look at the interactions that arise from the work to see a network in process, the pattern of who talks to whom how often. Trust develops and relationships crystallize in interactions over time and in moments of crisis. New communication technologies stimulate new forms of organization and induce change, planned or not, desired or not.

*Warnings: From Isolation to Overload.* A lack of links is a clear cause of network failure. Missing physical connections, interactions that peter out, and stillborn relationships plague every network. No true network will form where personal connections are weak, where people are not close. There is no trust without real relationships, and without trust there is no network.

The failures caused by too many links, too many messages, too quick a pace are less obvious. Overload is a major and widespread problem of the Information Age. You're in trouble when you dread calling into your voice mail or checking your e-mail because you know that once you begin you're committed for the next few hours. Clogged communications systems shoot overload to first place on the failure indicator list for fast-growing networks. Overload depresses learning, which is central to the Information Age organization. The well-functioning teamnet manages information dynamically—filtering, categorizing, storing, sharing, and updating it, offering interpretation just in time and without great hassle.

4. *Climbing Through the Teamnet Vines:* Fewer bosses, more leaders.

Everyone is a leader at the time when his or her unique experience and knowledge adds to the group's intelligence. Bell Atlantic's CEO Raymond W. Smith describes leadership on "ever-shifting, cross-disciplinary teams determined by who's most expert on the matter—not the corporate hierarchy."[2] That networks have multiple leaders surprises many people.

All human organizations have leaders, whether informal or formal. Hierarchy and bureaucracy minimize leadership; teamnets maximize it.

When Hyatt Hotels' sales and marketing organization went from functions to market segments, it appointed two leaders for each new market team. Each person holds a separate portfolio of responsibilities within the team. Everyone has something vital to contribute with leadership broadly distributed.

Consider these questions to gauge whether you have fewer bosses and more leaders: Do you hear only one voice at meetings? Are there subgroups with task leaders? Does more than one person make commitments and take responsibility? Do people feel heard and that they have a voice in decision making? Do they participate—or at least feel that they can? This sense of participation is a key indicator of teamnet health.

Look for new styles of leadership. In particular, look for the natural networkers, the coordinators. These are the people at the nexus of relationships, people who are natural catalysts. They constantly develop matches between people's needs and resources.

*Warnings: From Leaderless to Followerless.* Without many leaders networks fail, so it is easy to see how this spread-out organization could suffer from a lack of leadership. The "leaderless network" problem often creeps up slowly, almost undetected as the original crop of leaders burns out before new leaders are ready to come on line. Suddenly one day, the energy is gone and no one knows why.

An abundance of leaders can bring its own problems. The "prima donna" effect is a good name for the other extreme. Experts come in, do their thing, and leave while bosses breeze by dropping orders and special interests focus only on their own niches. If we're all leaders but none of us has learned to follow, we have a power struggle on our hands. Incessant squabbles paralyze the network. Leading and following is a dance; step on as few toes as possible, please. Heed the motto that Hyatt Hotel put on T-shirts: "Teamnet: It's an attitude."

5. *The Hierarchy and the Lower-archy:* Teamnets are naturally clumpy and clustered.

Contrary to popular belief, a network is not two-dimensional. Small groups, forming and reforming, make up big networks. Even the smallest networks carry out work in subgroups of one, two, or three. The word "teamnet" carries connotations of this multilevel reality: networks of teams of people.

Groups within groups nest internally in some teamnets. Arthur Andersen & Company's Business Systems Consulting group (BSC) comprises 765 consultants spread around the world in eighty locations housing two to forty-five people each helping small-to-medium-sized businesses install technology networks to meet business needs. The teams are local; the network is global.

Externally, teamnets are open organizations that evolve along with their environments. So it is equally important to consider the larger context. Teamnets may be part of a larger enterprise, or part of an industry, market, or movement—a hierarchy of levels.

We tend to network at our own level, where it is easiest to establish peer relationships, ignoring the other levels at our peril.

*Warnings: From No Uplinks to No Downlinks.* It's easy to lose touch with the hierarchy. But it's very dangerous. Many a promising teamnet effort has succeeded briefly, then shriveled and died because it lacked links to the senior levels of the company or to the stakeholder opinion leaders. In one dramatic case involving two companies, the vendor's executive committee killed a multihundred-million-dollar deal at the last minute because it was not briefed on the project until the moment of final decision. Often, problems with the hierarchy show up late in a change process rather than earlier when there is still time to address them. Remember: the hierarchy always has the last word.

It is just as dangerous to forget the ground floor where work takes place, the people at the operating levels who support the network's activities. The people on the front lines of production, such as Harry Brown's hourly workforce in Erie, Pennsylvania, and those in services, such as at the front desk of the Marriott in Jacksonville, need to network. Customers and suppliers need involvement up and down the line. Change is killed just as effectively from below as above. When people on the front line are out of touch they shield themselves from innovations launched from above, which causes unintended side effects.

## Up the Organizational Scale

New organizations are erupting at every level, from very small groups to globe-spanning networks. The dominant business phenomenon of the 1990s is networking, a much more flexible and fluid mode than its predecessors.

For instance, we are witnessing an explosion of new large-scale, multicorporate networks that offer both cooperation and competition in a veritable zoo of *strategic alliances*. Such alliances are true networks, where the independence of members is as clear and unquestioned as the inappropriateness of hierarchy. With the independence of members and multiple leadership as basic premises, the trick lies in creative development of joint purpose and voluntary relationships.

Two-party alliances are still the norm; multimember alliances are increasingly common. Small businesses also engage this fast-growing trend to ally in a big way. *Flexible business networks* are taking hold throughout the world, including the United States, some stimulated by government funds, countless others started by the companies themselves. These small company alliances offer a remarkable demonstration of the economic value of business links among independent companies.

Beyond the reach of individual firms are massive conglomerations of economic activity that are to some degree integrated and focused. These very-large-scale entities are likely to acquire increasing importance in the future. Known in Japan as *keiretsu,* they are linkages among a large number of firms in diverse industries anchored by a major bank or manufacturer. Massive webs of strategic alliances are now appearing elsewhere on the global stage. Global "digital keiretsu"—the eighteen companies that swirl around Toshiba, for example—are shaping the future convergence of computers, telecommunications, and media.

In short, teamnets surface at all levels of organizations. Some networks demonstrate the five teamnet principles better than others, but all reflect the principles to some degree. They are changing businesses and organizations of all sizes, everywhere.

### Notes

1. Remarks of Dee Hock, president and CEO emeritus of VISA International, at a meeting convened by the Joyce Foundation on Oct. 11, 1993. We thank Joel Getzendanner of the Joyce Foundation and Rebecca Adamson, founder of First Nations Financial Institute, for introducing us to Hock's work.

2. Raymond W. Smith, "Bell Atlantic's Virtual Work Force," *The Futurist* (Mar.–Apr. 1994, p. 13).

# Novell's Ten-Thousand-Piece Puzzle

## Terri Holbrooke

Although working at a dynamic company such as Novell was exciting, I used to believe until very recently that someday we would become a "grown-up company." My colleagues and I hoped that when Novell matured we would have nice organizational charts, a clearly defined hierarchy, well-defined policies, and the other trappings of a well-managed corporation.

But the more I understand the changes underway in business today, the more I realize that this dream of growing up and becoming a real company is misplaced. Instead, I have come to think that all the grown-up companies we have been admiring for so long should operate the way Novell does. In fact, I now believe that Novell is a marvelous example of a revolutionary form that is being called a "network organization."

It has been so natural for Novell to operate in this networking type of business environment that, like most people who participate in a revolution of some kind, we didn't really know we were in the middle of one at all. However, with all the management experts

---

Terri Holbrooke was senior vice president of international marketing at Novell/WordPerfect Corporation at the time these events occurred. She is now senior vice president of worldwide marketing at Ziff-Davis Publishing Company, San Francisco.

recently discussing this great advance in terms of diagrams, examples of network organizations, and how they operate, I am amazed to find myself thinking, "Oh yeah, that's what we do. Hmm. I always thought we just operated that way by accident. What a smart way to run a business!"

Because Novell recently passed through a difficult but instructive experience when we merged with WordPerfect, I think it would be interesting to examine this merger and the reason it failed. It's a great case study that highlights the differences between traditional corporate structures and the type we have developed at Novell.

## The Novell-WordPerfect Merger: A Case Study in Organizational Opposites

When we announced our intention to merge with WordPerfect, a flurry of press coverage immediately pointed out how smart or how stupid this merger was (sometimes from the same people on different days). The merger was consummated in June of 1994 when we paid $1.4 billion for WordPerfect, and at the same time paid $145 million to acquire the Quattro Pro spreadsheet from Borland.

The prevailing wisdom at the time was summed up by a reporter from the *Guardian* (we had this quote posted on a wall in my department because it's so hilarious), who said, "Combining these firms should be easy because their headquarters are only a couple of miles apart." The logic of this view of our world went something like this: both companies have roughly the same number of employees and the same revenue, both have products enjoying strong market share, they have different and complementary niches in the software industry, and, of course, they are just ten miles apart, which always helps.

But for those of us on the inside of this merger, it actually felt more like a struggle to unite opposites. WordPerfect was a privately held company; Novell was a public company. WordPerfect had never been through a merger or acquisition before; Novell had gone through fifteen different acquisitions and mergers and had made major investments in nine other firms. WordPerfect was centralized at one site; Novell was decentralized both organizationally and geographically. We may have said that our formal headquarters are in Utah because we wanted to create the illusion of being located someplace, but much of our management was spread across the west and east coasts. So actually it is more realistic to say that Novell operates out of a "virtual headquarters," which we believe lies somewhere over Winnemucca, Nevada.

From a product standpoint, Novell's Netware is a kind of "background product"; most people using information networks are probably using Novell networks and don't know it. The people who buy those networks are very technically oriented; they do IT for a living and compose a small audience. So we had a very high-priced, low-volume product that was sold to the technical marketplace. WordPerfect, however, had a very low-priced, high-volume product that was sold to those of you who use word processing, often in a retail setting.

Very different approach to marketing, very different approach to the customer. Even the word customer meant very different things to our two companies. And because I come out of a graphic design and art background, the most important thing to me was that Novell's logo was red and WordPerfect's was blue, so this was never going to work. In Utah, this issue is fraught with meaning, since BYU is blue and the University of Utah is red.

Perhaps the most dramatic difference in the companies can be summed up in the contrast between hierarchical versus network structures. WordPerfect was a very traditional hierarchy. We had funny stories to tell that often reminded us of this clash as we brought these two organizations together.

There was a flurry of meetings and activities in Utah the week prior to the announcement. We on the Novell side went to WordPerfect for the first meeting and were told that we would meet in the executive boardroom. For those from hierarchical companies, this would not be unusual. But we Novell people looked at each other and said, "Executive boardroom! Well, won't this be interesting." We walked in and noted that they had real wood! A very big deal to Novell people.

Also, Ray Norda, our founder, was very big on offices that were all the same size; every office in Novell is exactly the same size, whether you are the president or a manager. We do have cubicles that are smaller, but if you graduate from a cubicle to an office, it never gets any better. That's it. At WordPerfect, not only were there cubicles and offices with wood, there were actually offices with bathrooms! Now here was a concept that was new to us.

As my group moved to the new headquarters on the Orem, Utah, campus where WordPerfect is located, a facilities manager came to me and said, "Now, in your building, there are two offices with bathrooms. I'd like to know who you would like to have the other office?" In other words, he assumed that I would want one of the offices with a bathroom. I said, "We have one handicapped employee, who is our librarian. It would be wonderful for her to have a bathroom close at hand." He looked quizzical. "And," I said, "As for the other office with a bathroom, let's make it a conference room, so that there's less interruption when someone has to leave momentarily." He replied, "But don't you . . . ? It's very important . . ." I said, "No, it's not important that I have an office with a bathroom; it's more important that I have an office as close as possible to the receptionist so that I can hear what calls are coming in and what customers are saying. I have to remain near the nervous system-control center of the department."

The most critical difference in the way these two companies worked lay in the way information is used. What we discovered in the course of this merger is that at WordPerfect information is held by those with power. It was shared through a very top-down-driven process, so that it flows through an elegant, complex path at appropriate times to appropriate people.

At Novell, information is networked. Information is just data until you share it enough that it becomes enriched with everybody else's input and turns into insight. Having information at your control is viewed rather with a jaded eye; if you've got the information, why haven't you spread it around so that it can come back to you in some better way? The idea among some managers that they "owned" their units and the people in them always struck us as wrong. Everybody "owned" everything at Novell, which caused us all to work together.

As we went through this merger, we found that the WordPerfect people would meet with their top management to explain something, and then management would come back to the employees with decisions. On our side, top management was whoever you could find in the lunchroom. You simply told them everything you knew, and they told you everything they knew. Everyone was constantly e-mailing everybody else who they thought needed to be kept informed. Ray Norda would send out e-mail messages across the company saying, "We are getting ready to develop a new program. Any of you who may have any interest ought to be in touch soon. We'd love to have any input you might offer."

So we had this very messy process going on over here, while they had this very organized process going on over there. The problem was that their organized process took so much longer than our catch-as-catch-can process that we were usually done with our work and waiting for them. We would typically arrive ready for the next integration meeting, but the WordPerfect side would still be struggling halfway through last week's process of moving information through its system.

Another area that revealed fascinating differences is in the way our two companies regarded job security. We had a total of ten thousand employees when we first joined the two companies, which is huge for a software operation. We went down to seven thousand in the first six months. This loss was not considered a negative thing from the standpoint of Novell employees because we all understood the need for dynamic change. WordPerfect employees had a more difficult time, although they seem to be adapting well to this shift in philosophy.

At Novell, change is viewed as ongoing; it is something you'd better initiate so it doesn't get done to you. Change is also seen as something that leads to opportunity. For example, my department went from more than five hundred down to three hundred. Of the hundred Novell people who left, 75 percent have started their own ventures and are making more money and having more fun; they are also looking more rested and more tanned then those of us who have stayed, I might add. The WordPerfect people floundered initially, but they caught on, and many of them are partnering with or working for some of the Novell people who went off to do their own thing.

So we had two dramatically different views of job security. At WordPerfect, there had never been a layoff or major restructuring; people were basically still in the same jobs they had held for years and years. At Novell, no one is usually in a job for more than a year before something changes; they may move into a new role, or we may have a layoff of some kind that releases some employees to other opportunities. Inevitably these people are sort of envied because they leave with a great package that gives them an opportunity to spend time starting something new and end up having a lot more fun.

Another area of difference was the amount of flexibility the two companies expected from their people. We were in an executive staff meeting discussing some planned trips to Europe and Asia when someone said we'll need to get back to you on this topic in a week because there are a number of employees who will be affected by this decision. One of the WordPerfect executives said, "But I'll be in Europe next week." The Novell people responded in unison, "So you'll be up late."

The view on the WordPerfect side was that work was a place; the Novell side thought work was an activity. Because WordPerfect people viewed work as a place, when you left that place you really couldn't work. Thus when you went to a sales meeting in Europe you could only do the sales meeting. And because Novell people viewed work as an activity, it went with you wherever you are. Our technology allowed us to stay as connected as you want to be. Sometimes this idea of work as a place is intriguing to me because I think that would be kind of nice. It was interesting to see Word-Perfect people come to grips with the fact that work is not a place, that they must remain accessible, log into the network to read their e-mail, and do their work wherever they are. Only in that way could the combined company continue to move ahead.

## Conclusion: Two Ways to Solve Puzzles

I originally titled this chapter "A Ten-Thousand-Piece Puzzle with No Easy Pieces" because this captures the essence of our experience. The Novell-WordPerfect merger required integrating ten thousand employees from vastly different corporations within six months into a fully functioning, highly competitive single organization. An intricate, unpredictable undertaking of this type can be accurately compared to the difficult task of assembling an especially complex puzzle. Using the puzzle analogy also helps us see that there seem to be two strikingly different approaches to accomplishing this challenge.

When I was growing up, every Christmas we would get a puzzle to solve as a family. By coincidence, there was a family living next to us that also got a puzzle to do every Christmas. Now, my father is in the military and I have one brother, so we had a small nuclear family of four people that approached our puzzle in a rather military-like, hierarchical fashion. But the family next door had eight kids and dozens of relatives hanging around all the time, so their puzzles were solved in a far more chaotic way.

At our house, the puzzle was always placed on the same table with two chairs, and if you wanted to work on the puzzle you had to have an open chair. If two people were already working on the puzzle, you had to wait. Further, the puzzle was done in a very organized fashion. You first found pieces for the corners, which could take hours just going through the box. The second job was to fill in the border. Only when these first two jobs were completed would you work on some inner section, and even then there was a rule that you were to look for pieces that could be identified by the color or pattern of the section being worked on. So when you sat down at the table you had to find out where we were we in the process and move ahead logically.

Of course, growing up in this family it seemed perfectly normal to me. However, I noticed that the people next door did not use a "puzzle table," but worked wherever in the house they happened to be sitting. Also, sometimes six or seven people would be working on the puzzle at the same time. Some were looking for corners, some just found three or four pieces that fit together, and some thought they'd like to do a border. Although they worked in this very chaotic way, their puzzle always got done before ours. It made me mad because we were so much better organized!

Well, as we went through this merger with WordPerfect I kept seeing this same clash between two different ways of working on a puzzle: the highly organized, top-down process versus the chaotic approach in which everybody does his piece his own way. The insight I gained out of this analogy explains why our merger failed ultimately. All the differences I've noted boiled down to this: Word-Perfect only knew how to solve puzzles in the laborious, hierarchical method, whereas Novell was good at solving puzzles using organized chaos.

We tried very hard to combine these different corporate cultures by drawing on both methods. The idea was that the role of executive management would be to provide an orderly framework to work within, and the role of the rank and file would be to accomplish our goals any way they could within this framework. We knew it would be messy, but by doing both at the same time it could be productive.

In terms of our puzzle analogy, executives "worked on the corners." We spent many months in exotic off-site meetings thinking through our proposed goals and values for the combined company. After we were done, we announced the following goals for the merger: we need to build new markets; we need to be more global; we need to focus our product development efforts from the initial 160 products between our two companies to fewer than 50; and we need to improve revenue per employee through layoffs.

At the same time, top management told employees, "Fill in the borders of this puzzle by drawing on your strengths." We also told employees that we needed to maintain our core competencies, the strengths that Novell and WordPerfect both shared: great customer loyalty. Great employee pride. Fabulous pattern of partnering. And coopetition, a term Ray Norda coined a couple of years ago to describe balancing the need to compete and cooperate at the same time with the same people.

While the executives were busy doing this, however, the employees were busy getting together to create the new Novell. When we came back from our off-site meetings to communicate these goals and core strengths that we needed to maintain, we found that employees had already been getting together in groups, working on pieces of the puzzle. They would typically say, "Look, we found five pieces that fit together. We don't know where they fit in the final picture, but we've accomplished that part of puzzle. Let's continue and get everyone to meet with their counterparts in the other company."

The success of this combined approach convinced me of the need for both a hierarchical and networking approach to management. Some overall strategic framework, common corporate systems, and other such broad forms of hierarchical organization are essential to frame the problem, but the best way to actually solve it is to allow a large number of talented people almost complete freedom to go about it as they think best. In other words, top management should lay out the corners and border and then let the organization fill in the rest of the puzzle.

This approach may have worked fine under ordinary circumstances, but the Novell-WordPerfect merger hardly took place under ordinary circumstances. As I've noted, we had to complete this ten-thousand-piece puzzle perfectly and almost immediately because the entire software industry was undergoing an upheaval. Fierce competitors were introducing powerful new products almost daily in an attempt to win the race of building the information networks of the future. In short, there were no "easy pieces" that you usually count on to achieve that crucial breakthrough in completing a puzzle.

Despite the great progress both sides made in overcoming these deep structural differences, we were unable to unify our operations smoothly enough to surmount growing competition from Microsoft's introduction of various networking products, such as Windows NT. The challenge of coordinating these two groups of employees and managers from very different corporate cultures hurt our combined efforts to bring new products out quickly and to market them effectively. For that reason, in February 1996 Novell had to reverse its merger decision by selling WordPerfect to Corel Corporation of Canada.

Some benefits were realized during this short marriage, however. WordPerfect is now comfortably integrated into a company where it can fit more easily, and its employees have learned how to operate in a more lean, dynamic fashion through their association with Novell. Also, Novell retained some units of WordPerfect that fit strategically into its goals, such as the groupware unit that is perfectly suited to Novell's current efforts to improve its networking systems. But the reality is that this failed merger cost Novell a loss estimated at $750 million. That is a large sum for a company like Novell, and it drives home the huge importance of understanding these crucial differences in the way modern corporations work.

# 10

# Managing the Virtual Organization

*at Telepad*

Ron Oklewizc

T he concept of managing a virtual organization is well accepted now, but I don't think many people really understand how to put this idea into actual practice. That is what we have done at Telepad for the past few years with great success.

When we first started to work this way, we had no idea what a virtual organization was until a reporter from *Business Week* called one day to tell us, "You are a model of the virtual corporation." I asked, "What's that?"

It turns out we had invented this system without realizing it because it is essential to survive in today's competitive business environment. Every manager now knows that the Information Revolution is intensifying competition, but so far we have seen just the beginning. Only 2 percent of business information is digitized as yet, and the information economy will not really take off until business is digitized end-to-end.

---

Ron Oklewizc, president and CEO of Telepad Corporation, founded the company in 1990 after a successful career managing new ventures at Xerox, Apple, and other great computer companies. While manager of Apple's Federal Systems Division, he increased revenues from $3 million to $100 million in five years. In 1994, *Business Week* featured Telepad as a model of the virtual corporation.

The problem we faced at Telepad was typical of small firms: How can a little company like ours survive in this racing global economy? Telepad does a fine job as a total systems integrator, but we only have thirty employees. How could we possibly match the enormous skills and assets of IBM, Apple, and Microsoft?

What we have learned is that size and assets are not really the most crucial factors in today's economy. In an age of exploding change, the most critical advantage is to be first in the market with a superior product. The ability to quickly enlist the talents and assets of others in a bold new venture is extremely important because it offers a flexibility and agility that big firms can't offer precisely because they are so large.

That is the great advantage of a virtual organization. This revolutionary concept views a venture as an open-ended set of possibilities, limited only by our ability to understand the customer's changing needs and to organize a network of business partners that can help serve those needs. Understanding the power of this idea and putting it into practice to solve actual problems has been the key to our success.

I would like to describe our experiences briefly to highlight the reality of the virtual organization rather than the theory. My focus is on what we have learned to be the single most important aspect of this concept: forming effective working relationships with a great variety of business partners.

## Marriage Versus Dating

The most important thing to know is the type of partner you are working with. Before we understood this we treated all alliances the same, thinking they were all "virtual relationships": the partner who was doing our manufacturing, the partner who was investing cash in the company, and those who were marketing our products. It was a disaster. You simply have to understand the nature of these different relationships and classify them into different groups.

It may sound strange, but business partners can be best understood if we compare them to sexual partners. Like the relationships formed between men and women, alliances can take two different forms: marriage and dating.

Our dating partners are subject matter experts; these are people who have special knowledge that we bring in for temporary purposes. For instance, we may partner with the developer of some software solution, and it gets a royalty for its contribution. We develop and write the program, but it provides the subject matter expertise. We have successfully conducted this type of relationship with dating partners such as Microsoft, Sun, and a few other firms that are subject matter experts in operating systems and components.

In contrast, a marriage partner is critical to the supply chain because it adds unique value, necessitating a permanent relationship. For instance, IBM is our manufacturing partner. When we first signed a contract with IBM, we thought, "This is going to be neat. We can use all their manufacturing and computer skills, and all we have to do is learn how to put their people to work. Instead of struggling to build computers in a garage, we could take this big elephant into the garage and walk him around teaching him how to do it for us." Well, it didn't turn out that way because the elephant had a mind of his own, as I will explain shortly. That was our first tough experience with marriage partners, and we learned a great deal from it.

The central role of a virtual corporation is to offer a shared vision that holds all these relationships together. It is almost impossible to partner successfully with somebody that does not find your vision attractive. If the partner sees the relationship as an odd source of revenue or some other expedient advantage, either run for the hills or try to explore what it is truly interested in. A partnership will not work if the other firm's primary goal is to make money because this is not just about making money. You have got to find important reasons why you are in this together before trouble arises. Of course, every partner will prefer to engage in a secure venture, particularly if you can gain the type of competitive advantage once enjoyed by Apple or Motorola. But that is not very common today.

The first thing to focus on is forming a contractual agreement. If you do not have a firm contract and a strong personal sense of bonding, the venture will almost certainly encounter massive problems. So it is essential to have both of these ties established before moving ahead. Both partners have to share the same common goal and vision and be willing to put their agreement to paper. My advice is to hire a marriage counselor—a broker of some sort—because you will need one. It is essential to understand both sides of the relationship and resolve any differences, and that can be best done through a third party.

It is also important to anticipate conflict because it is almost inevitable. You cannot just assume that the relationship is going to work out fine. A virtual organization is a dynamic undertaking, so you have got to accept the fact that unforeseen events will alter the relationship, the partners' interests may change, and many other difficulties will arise. This is even more difficult because the key to making a virtual organization work is getting the product to market fast, so you have to resolve any problems quickly.

For instance, our elephant—IBM—decided that he was going to sit down one day. The IBM executive in charge of our venture said, "We don't operate the way Telepad does. You guys work twenty-four hours a day, your engineers sleep in their offices during product debugging trials, they eat pizza and throw them around the lab, with music blasting all the time. IBM doesn't run like that. We work eight hours a day, no music is allowed in the labs, and you can't find pizza laying around. My engineers are upset."

Cultural clashes of this type have to be respected. There are myriad such differences that can cause serious product delays. You have got to be able to work through disagreements by making sure that the role of each partner is clearly defined and that sound communications are ongoing. This leads me to my next major point.

## Build a Trusting Relationship

Success for us is managing our partners, not technical wizardry. The first discipline we have learned to respect is that we are responsible for the relationship, not the partner. If we can't make sure all these relationships will work, then we will not be able to retain our customer's patronage.

The critical nature of maintaining a loyal, trusting relationship is highlighted by another problem we had with IBM. I had just resolved the cultural clash between our engineers when IBM decided to take away one of our prized customers. Now, the IBM manager who was our partner did not do this. It was another division. But because of our successful relationship with the customer, we were able to resolve the problem. I offered a better solution, and it turned out that the IBM division that was competing with us was partially right and we were partially right. So we came up with a combined solution that was accepted, and we regained the contract. The customer felt we had been treating them well, so they reciprocated by treating us well.

The reason for this happy ending is that we considered the relationship with this customer to be a marriage type of partnership. We saw them as a true partner sharing a common destiny. We allowed them into our development organization, invited them to inspect our product design and development operations all the way down the line. They would come down and have pizza with us as we built their product. That solid sense of commitment saved the relationship.

That lesson also caused us to divide our company into segments, and then have each segment focus on serving its customers, understanding the customers' expectations, and guaranteeing them satisfaction. I mean really guaranteeing it. We have a "no-fault" guarantee system. If a Telepad machine is run over by a truck (to take an extreme case), the client can just give us the name tag and we will send a new machine. We realize the customer has a field force of highly paid workers who need our equipment in order to be up and running, so we have to get them back into operations somehow. We can't argue about what has happened. We have to get the customer operating.

This is helped by providing constant two-way information up and down the line, tailoring the product to deliver the best possible value, and ensuring flawless quality. The competitive edge in all of this does not lie in technical innovation primarily. It lies in packaging all these complex working relationships together into a total customer solution.

Most of our products must be delivered quickly because the client needs a solution instantaneously. For example, we are working with Sikorsky Helicopter, which has been a good customer of ours for a long time and is now becoming a marriage partner. Our machines plug right into their helicopters to analyze and diagnose the chopper's performance and pinpoint any faults. If a problem is discovered, a Sikorsky interactive electronic technical manual comes online and tells the maintenance person exactly what is wrong with that helicopter. He or she then selects parts that need to be replaced and does the work.

That entire process is also communicated wirelessly back to Sikorsky and Telepad, and the diagnostic information goes to the designers who built the product. In this way, all parties understand immediately that a faulty design feature is causing problems in the helicopters and that a redesign is needed. So we are, in effect, redesigning the product at the very time we service it. That is what a virtual organization is all about. This is a great example of how a strong set of dynamic working relationships can be mobilized and deployed instantly to accomplish something that is urgently needed.

So carefully managing the relationships among our partners, subcontractors, customers, and even our competitors is the key to our success.

Let me offer another good example by describing what happened when our elephant decided to roll over on us. One day, IBM changed the management of the division we worked with without our knowledge. A new controller came in and decided that he needed to make his fourth-quarter goals, so he ordered the division to sell off its excess inventory to solve the problem. Well, I came down to their shop and found that some of our vital components had been sold. I am embarrassed to say that this took me by complete surprise.

We resolved the misunderstanding, but this highlights the need to stay on top of details in a virtual venture. If you do not inspect things daily, the project can run away from you as your partners change goals, particularly when new people come into play. Somebody must be in charge of making sure the relationship will work. A "product champion" must manage every venture to ensure that any obstacles that pop up are surmounted and that all the other countless things are done to carry a project through to its successful completion. A virtual organization is not a fantasy or a gimmick. It is an incredible amount of hard work to provide the leadership for creating close teamwork between suppliers, employees, customers, and management based on agreements, trust, training, good ideas, rewards, and sound decision making.

Good human resources management (HRM) is an important part of this task. To be assured that our employees are giving us their best, we have implemented employee stock purchase plans and a bonus system. These incentives are a silent guiding force that coordinates operations. Everybody in the company receives a bonus based on their average revenue and expenses. Employees set three goals that they choose themselves. The only thing we ask is that they coordinate their goals with the company's goals. Every quarter, employees set their separate goals. They then self-inspect their performance and decide whether they made their targets or not.

The most important benefit we give employees is good training. This is a gift of lasting value because it makes them employable elsewhere.

We also guide these HRM practices by benchmarking. We learn who our best competitors are and then make sure that our human resources practices are at least as good as theirs.

Without the virtual organization, Telepad would never have succeeded. The fact is that modern economies are starting to develop product customization beyond belief, which means dramatic gains are essential in speed of design, manufacture, and delivery. These huge advances in performance are only possible if we redefine how business works in a fundamental way. The key idea is to learn how to work together more quickly, easily, and flexibly—in other words, to operate as a virtual organization.

# Part III

# Leveraging Knowledge with an
# Intelligent Infrastructure

*Producing Learning Orgs.*
*&*
*Intelligent Orgs.*

# 11

# Our Vision of the Information Superhighway

## Raymond W. Smith

I n America today we are witnessing what the great economist
Joseph Schumpeter called "creative destruction," a revolutionary
process of innovation that destroys the existing economic order and
replaces it with a new, more robust order. Communication technology has emerged as the world's most powerful agent of change.

The effects of information technology on our new economy will
be revolutionary in the truest sense. For instance, the common
materials used to produce today's technological advances—metal,
sand, and air—are less than 2 percent of the total costs of production. The other 98 percent resides in the value of knowledge.
George Gilder calls this "the overthrow of matter," the most fundamental feature of today's information economy. In the Industrial
Age, wealth derived from raw materials, geography, size, and other

Raymond W. Smith has been called the "father of the Information Age."
He is chairman and CEO of Bell Atlantic Corporation. Bell Atlantic and
its new partner NYNEX are the second-largest communications operator
in the United States, covering thirteen eastern seaboard states and twenty-
six million customers owning 30 percent of the nation's wealth. Smith and
his associates are planning a variety of new alliances and ventures to pursue his company's goal of creating a full-service international communications network.

physical attributes. In the Information Age, wealth is a function of information, vision, and other properties of the mind.

Software over hardware, mind over matter. Knowledge is supplanting raw material as the primary economic resource.

In fact, new technologies are increasing productivity to such an extent that we can no longer measure the effect of technological investment on growth using traditional yardsticks. That's because the relationship between knowledge and productivity is nonlinear. Unlike raw materials such as coal or iron, knowledge is a resource you can't use up. The more of it you dispense in an organization, the more you generate. This is what I call the "loaves and fishes" property of communications. Unlike the old economic law of diminishing returns that governed an Industrial Age, we can now enjoy expanding returns in an Information Age.

As you may know, Moore's Law states that microprocessors double in power every eighteen months, while costs fall by half. With power increasing exponentially, it's easy to see how traditional measures of productivity go out the window. During the past decade this trend has driven the economics of the computer industry, leading to today's fully distributed, mainframe-on-every-desk phenomenon.

If Moore's Law is the law of the microchip, Metcalfe's Law is the law of the network. Named for the inventor of Ethernet, Metcalfe's Law states that a network's value grows in proportion to the number of users and information sources connected to it. To cite an extreme example, how valuable would your phone be if you could call only one person? Not very. But hook your phone up to a worldwide network and its value grows enormously. Substitute "computer" for "phone" in this illustration, and you get an idea of what will drive the economics of our industry for the rest of the decade; substitute "television" and you get the same answer.

These trends make it easy to see why our information infrastructure is so critical to the success of companies, governments, schools, families, and the entire social system. The emerging world of communications promises to transform virtually every aspect of life in the next several years.

Let me offer you our vision of what the information superhighway will be like and how it will transform the way we live. Throughout this chapter, I'll also discuss the workplace and society—how information technology has changed not only how we do things, but also the very essence of what we do.

## Defining the Information Superhighway

Let's start with the infrastructure itself. Who are the main characters involved in its construction? Well, Bell Atlantic, for one. Together with our new partner, NYNEX, we will invest some $5 billion a year to upgrade our network. But there are many other actors in this play as well. When you consider the convergence of the computer, television, telephone, motion picture, publishing, retail, and gaming industries, the cast of characters is enormous.

Even the information infrastructure itself is a pluralist concept, evolving not from one network but from a symphony of many interoperable networks. Digitalization enables users to access a robust broadband system from virtually any technology platform. We also envision completely open systems. I define *open networks* as those that, in addition to offering their own content, provide the capability for others to do the same.

The Internet, for instance, has soared in popularity because it embodies software protocols that are compatible with all types of PCs and networks. It's virtually impossible to overstate the growth of the Internet—Web sites doubling every few weeks, users growing at double-digit rates month after month. 1995, I believe, will go down in history as the year of the Internet, the year "Net Fever" spawned instant millionaires.

The exploding success of the Internet symbolizes a crucial shift in our view of the information superhighway: from a hardware-software paradigm to a network-centric paradigm. In a converging world, the network is the very taproot of growth, the source of nourishment for the computer, entertainment, and communication fields.

Metcalfe's Law identifies how interactivity gives a network its value—by providing content and applications just in time, on demand. Proof that the law is now in force lies in the fact that users crave not only more processing power but more connectivity. It's estimated that as much as 80 percent of Microsoft's Office Suite software goes unused. Today, users are hungry for connectivity, bandwidth, and faster response times.

This vision has also been validated recently by historic changes in telecommunication regulations that initiated one of the most exciting periods in our industry. The long-awaited Telecommunications Act of 1996 is now law, and a new cycle of economic growth, investment, and innovation has begun. More companies can now vie with one another for shares of the local, long distance, and video markets. As the pie expands and the number of contenders increases, countless new opportunities for suppliers, partners, and allies will emerge.

It's important, however, to put legislation in its proper perspective. Significant as the new law may be, it pales in comparison to the market forces that have been shaping our destinies all along— the profound changes in business and consumer demand resulting from the digitalization of information.

## Emerging Information Services

Now, what exactly will this highway do? The short answer is that it will provide a wealth of information services connecting people around the world into a single interactive community.

There has been a great deal of controversy over this prospect. Many analysts claimed a public that has trouble programming its VCRs will never take to digital TV offering interactive services. Their argument was that, in a world of couch potatoes, interactive multimedia is all hype; there won't be a mass of users and there won't be killer applications. At the other extreme, many believed that PCs will dominate home information systems.

But the answer to the question of whether digital TV or the PC will win acceptance in the home market is simple: yes. Both will find increasing use for different purposes. Recent developments suggest that easy-to-use, affordable consumer products like the WebTV will connect people to the Internet via their TV sets, whereas the PC may soon be able to receive broadcast video. So I see a huge parallel market emerging.

I think we can declare the interactive TV debate officially closed. The truth is, consumers do want interactivity. Our interactive TV market trial has showed us that video-on-demand outperforms pay-per-view almost nine to one (comparing ratios of videos viewed to number of subscribers). Leading national retailers participating in the trial came away convinced that interactive shopping works. It is the future.

Against that background, then, here are my views on how the mass market for interactive services will develop. This is not a prediction so much as one person's five planning assumptions:

1. We will continue to see growth in the market for powerful networked personal computers.

2. We will also see the simultaneous development of a low-cost digital networked appliance that will power a large-screen TV, a PC-style display unit, or, probably, both.

3. We will see more intelligence residing in servers and in the network itself.

4. We will see networks delivering high-capacity transmission, instant connections, and point-to-point communications—all coming faster and cheaper than most experts predict.

5. And we will find that customers won't care how they get their information services—as long as the network delivers them in a compelling, low-cost, secure, and easy-to-use way.

Note that in all five assumptions, "network" is the operative word. At Bell Atlantic, we are seeing a surge of demand for network services of various sorts. In 1996, more than 15 percent of households in our region had more than one phone line; we expect penetration of second lines to grow to 35 to 40 percent by the end of the decade. In ISDN—where Bell Atlantic accounts for a third of this country's installed base—lines in service grew to more than two hundred thousand. And finally, our fast-packet business showed double-digit growth in 1996.

The lesson is that there are huge opportunities for companies who can find a new growth model, and that shouldn't be too difficult. After all, nine out of ten Americans have never "logged on," two-thirds of home computers aren't connected to a network of any kind, and—except for a few trials—every television set in America is still a one-way receiver.

So how do we feed the growing demands of telecommuters, netsurfers, and knowledge workers—and bring interactive services to a mass market at the same time? The optimal network will have four basic characteristics:

1. *Flexibility.* Telecommuters, cyber-shoppers, videoconferees and Net surfers tend to do more than one of these things at once, so it's important that the network be able to accommodate them all.

2. *Universality.* These applications require connectivity that's available anywhere in the world.

3. *Switchability.* Any broadband network will support one-way access to a database, but only switchable networks—that is, those that let you communicate point-to-point in either direction—will support teleconferencing.

4. *Standards.* Connectivity must be standardized if it is to be a truly anywhere-to-anywhere proposition.

Flexibility, universality, switchability, and standards. This is why cable networks will remain behind the curve. Cable modems—if they ever get to market—may be fast, but they're not standardized, they have limited two-way capabilities and they're not available everywhere.

But local carriers are in a unique position to meet the entire spectrum of emerging customer requirements for bandwidth and connectivity. That's why we have been pumping bandwidth into the Bell Atlantic network for several years. We've digitized all our central offices, put SONET rings in all major business loops, and installed more fiber miles than anyone but AT&T, including nearly 100 percent of our interoffice lines. We've moved aggressively in this arena on several fronts:

- To provide fast, high-capacity transmission that all these applications need, we've taken steps to introduce ISDN to a mass market. ISDN delivers data thirteen times faster than phone lines and four times faster than today's fastest modems. Bell Atlantic and NYNEX currently have more than 330,000 ISDN lines operating for business subscribers, and we are also introducing the best-priced residential ISDN product in the nation, making it available everywhere in our region. We just signed an agreement to market ISDN via the Microsoft Network that comes with every version of Windows 95 and Windows NT, and, in concert with U.S. Robotics, we've just announced a family of low-priced ISDN products.
- In 1997 we introduced ADSL data connections, which are even faster—"ISDN on steroids." These lines will have speeds of 1.5 megabits per second downstream and 64 kilobits upstream and a dedicated ten-base T Ethernet LAN connection, and the ability to use existing network interface devices for hooking up customers. In 1997, we'll be ready to deploy VDSL, with 6 to 10 megabits downstream and 644 kilobits upstream speed, suitable for even the most challenging real-time full-motion video as well as two-way video or data transmission.
- Also in 1997, we began migrating to the ultimate information-age platform—broadband to the customer—in our best markets.

This transformation will include deployment of ATM fast-packet switching, making our network the high-speed transport system for virtually any digital cargo. With its ability to mix data and video at any variable speed on a single copper wire, ATM renders moot the long-running debate over whether the PC or the TV will be the appliance of choice for interactive uses.

Our goal is to optimize our network for the whole range of communications—voice, video, data—and the whole range of terminals—TVs, PCs, Web stations, and, oh yes, telephones. On the provider end of the interactive information stream, the key ingredient to profitable growth will be in marketing and packaging.

## Marketing and Packaging

The battle for the high-value customer isn't just a fight over who has the most bandwidth because the prize won't necessarily go to the competitor with the biggest "pipe." The winner will be the company that provides a retail package giving customers the best combination of low prices, high reliability, security, superior performance, fine customer support, easy-to-use navigational tools, and a full array of voice, video, and Internet access services.

The way to maximize profitability is to load as many recurring revenue streams on a fixed investment base as you can. The more arrows in the quiver, the better the package you bring to the customer. The key to doing this well is what I've called "branding, bonding, and bundling": subscribe to ISDN, get Internet access for free. Put together your own customized service from our shelves: local and long distance, wired and wireless phone service, Internet access and e-mail, basic cable and video-on-demand.

This is not rocket science—it's a straightforward business strategy to squeeze maximum value out of your asset base, like McDonald's adding breakfast items to their menu.

## Continually Reinventing Corporate Management

The ability to select information you want, when you want it is more than "show biz." It has tremendous implications for several entire industries, hundreds of corporations, and society itself. Successful companies of the future will be the ones who use information technologies strategically to maximize productivity, delivery, and overall closeness to their customers.

I can assure you that working life is a lot different than it was when I got my MBA and went to work for "the phone company." Even the name "phone company" sounds quaint now. Although the old Bell System approximated the institutional power of the Catholic Church, it has long since been broken apart because the assumptions on which my entire generation of managers built their careers have been destroyed by the Information Revolution.

In just a few short years, we've seen how basic technologies such as electronic mail have transformed the way business operates, enabling us to empower employees, streamline work processes, flatten hierarchies, and eliminate bureaucracy, while dramatically increasing speed and quality of output.

E-mail is just the beginning. With some of our business customers, we're developing applications such as database access from anywhere; PC-based videoconferencing; telecommuting; and mobile sales forces working from virtual offices. Office to office, person to person, network to network, anyplace to anyplace.

Nothing short of a wireless revolution has been taking place to enable the virtual office, staffed by mobile, self-reliant employees. The number of subscribers to cellular service is growing at 20–30 percent a year, meaning wireless telephones will be a mainstay communication tool very soon.

That's a big reason why NYNEX and Bell Atlantic decided to pool our domestic cellular properties, and why we formed a nationwide alliance with Air Touch and USWest. We want to give our customers seamless national coverage along with the ability to stay with a single carrier as they travel.

But there's more to the wireless lane of the information super-highway than just car phones and voice communications. Data, video, and interactive multimedia will soon be widely available over wireless. Bell Atlantic already has wireless data services that let you send and receive faxes, plug into the office computer, send e-mail messages, monitor remote alarm systems, locate trucks and packages, and much more.

For example, we're helping banks create virtual loan offices in which loans and mortgages can be originated on the road by virtue of mobile database access. By bringing the bank to the customer, banks can bring in more business with faster and more convenient service.

We're also helping far-flung companies reduce the number of steps in meeting customer requirements. Our advanced intelligent network can automatically direct incoming calls to the appropriate representative, technical expert, or branch location before they're even answered. What's more, the incoming number can be pro-grammed to summon customer records, enabling the representative to get at the heart of the inquiry quickly.

I think you sense where all this is leading. People who at one time simply took orders now have the tools to assume full control over meeting customer needs. Service becomes more personal, more complete. Advancing technology means better work processes and fewer, better educated workers.

What's more, broadband networks and fast-packet services are bringing high-volume data applications to the electronic meeting place by dramatically changing the economics of data transport. Organizations can now move huge amounts of data—in virtually any form—over public networks. The investment is minimal, whereas the impact on productivity, cycle time, and efficiency is enormous.

Internet working applications have given rise to the concept of "enterprise networks" of suppliers, customers, clients, and business partners. Teams of experts can turn out their product on-line—no approval delays, no Federal Express trucks, and total sign-off in hours rather than days.

One of the emerging workplace concepts enabled by these applications is what Bob Waterman calls "adhocracy," in which teams of people step out of the traditional hierarchy, come together to get the job done, then move on to another—often very different—assignment. Management is thus reinvented continually.

## Looking to an Exciting Future

The same network capabilities will take us to interactive multimedia personal services delivered over your PC or television. These services will permanently change the nature of merchandising, medicine, education, and more.

Very soon, the entire shopping experience will be possible online—from consultation with a sales clerk, to opening a suit jacket, to reading the care label, to keying in your credit card number. The system will be shopper-driven, meaning you won't have to wait all night long for your favorite cubic zirconia to float across the screen. You see and investigate only what you want, at a time that's convenient for you.

By studying consumer behavior on the information superhighway, advertisers will be able to achieve unprecedented pinpoint accuracy and cost efficiency. Advertising itself will begin to take the form of in-depth infomercials accessed at the demand of the information-hungry shopper.

In the health care field, providers have already recognized the role information technology can play in delivering quality care to more people at lower cost. On-line patient monitoring is already a reality, as are visual consultations among patients, primary physicians, and specialists.

And in education, two-way remote classroom instruction, access to electronic text and video libraries, and multimedia databases are creating a true classroom without walls, where invigorated students take charge of learning while teachers do less lecturing and more guiding.

In short, the information superhighway is creating brand-new paradigms for living, working, learning, and even thinking. So we indeed stand on the brink of a tremendously creative phase in our industry. I can't tell you how delighted I am to be a part of this revolution that's really only just beginning.

# 12

# Taking a Byte Out of Bureaucracy

## David Walters

The title of my chapter highlights the great improvements we have made in the state government of Oklahoma by reorganizing the way we process information and communications—we've taken a "byte" out of bureaucracy.

## The Need for Improved Information and Communication

When I took office we were faced with a state government that operated a $7 billion budget, had 125,000 employees, and managed 168 agencies spread throughout a state of 69,000 square miles and seventy-seven counties. We also had, like any other state government, a number of remote locations and a variety of different

After a successful career in business, David Walters was elected Oklahoma's twenty-fourth governor in 1990. During his administration, the state led the nation in applying information technology to reform government, increase jobs, and improve education—all without a tax increase. One especially visible result was to create the largest state telemedicine system in America. Governor Walters graduated from the University of Oklahoma and obtained an MBA from Harvard University.

services. The difficulty was that communications were not well-organized and there was no good way to share information. Just a simple act of communicating to my staff and my cabinet was very cumbersome.

So we initiated a process of redesigning the way we deal with the huge load of diverse information required to manage state legislation, budgets, and finances. We also adopted e-mail and an internal networking system using Lotus Notes groupware to communicate in a far more convenient, faster way with all other players involved in state government.

Now you might say that e-mail is no big deal because it is a common technology now. But to make full use of it and to really encourage its utilization within state government has had a remarkable impact. Let me give you a simple example of a cabinet officer wanting to communicate with me. If he or she sent a letter, it was dictated, typed, mailed, delivered to the right person on my staff, reviewed, sent to me for a response, and then retraced the same entire process to get back to the cabinet officer. That process could take two weeks. So I simply told my cabinet officers that if they would e-mail me I would respond within twenty-four hours. The result was a massive adoption of e-mail because people like to have much more rapid, direct interaction.

We also found that the global broadcasting features of e-mail are a fine way to keep a wide number of people involved and active in our electronic discussions. We could pose a question and set a deadline for responses, and have far more information very quickly with which to make sound decisions. I could also more quickly respond to requests from a variety of agencies around the states. Now, that's just e-mail.

The system we established in Oklahoma will transmit any database anyone cares to put on it. We made very active use of common Rolodex files, common legislative tracking databases, and common budget information. When I was developing a $7 billion budget, the budget analyst for each area of state government and the legislative committee could directly discuss it with me and I could ask for more information, all electronically, saving countless individuals an enormous amount of time. Project management became very refined. We could outline a task, ask for responses, and keep a record of how the project was going in a very efficient and effective way.

We later put all of our information on the Internet using the Mosaic system. Now you can dial up Oklahoma's home page and look at an index to retrieve any type of information about our state very easily: the line item budget, all the arts and entertainment schedules in Oklahoma, and so on. We advertised our Internet address, so we received a growing volume of communication from state constituencies. Most media are now on the Internet, so we frequently engaged in a "running press conference" in which newspaper and TV journalists got on the Oklahoma Press Association Electronic Bulletin Board and asked us about press releases, for clarification of policy, and the like. We recently connected into fifty local Chamber of Commerce systems. If I wanted to see the prospects they are considering for various industries and economic sectors throughout Oklahoma, I could just pull up that address, browse around their Web site, and put in my two cents' worth.

With these various types of communication going on, we seem to have entered a new form of steady dialog that continues. You can probably imagine what happens when the Governor enters a Web site to ask the president of a Chamber of Commerce in Ardmore, Oklahoma, about some prospect. It certainly gets everybody's attention on the system. So there's a lot of play back and forth. We are not yet at the point where people can just sit before a television set, pick through Internet menus, and ask a high volumes of questions, but the opportunity to communicate back and forth is there.

This vastly improved ability for lateral communication began to resolve our major problem of increasing bureaucracy due to the proliferation of middle management. I consider myself a progressive Democrat, but I very strongly support term limits for this reason. Our political system may turn over a large portion of elected representatives in legislative bodies, but about 15 percent of them fundamentally lock up agencies for patronage purposes simply because they control them through the appropriations process or committee chairman process. It's not that Bill Clinton or I do not know how to reorganize executive agencies. The problem is that we don't have the power to do it.

However, the type of communication patterns I've just described mean that we should see more flexibility and more aggressive reform in the executive branch. As advanced technology encourages communication to become fast-paced and open, there has to be less of a pyramid. I started to get communications from second-tier staff members I needed to hear from. I couldn't talk with everybody, but I certainly broadened the scope of the people I interacted with and listened to because I could respond rapidly via e-mail. Agency managers can do the same thing. So this type of technology essentially flattens the organization.

## Information Technology Can Vastly Improve Government

What we found is that the pace of government action has speeded up and that we are able to do more with less. More importantly, we have been able to work with more limited resources and do an enormous amount of additional services for our public.

My budgets were reduced about 10 percent, my staff was reduced about 10 percent, and we cut the number of state employees for the first time in the history of the state, which is an enormous accomplishment. I think the governor's office became much more in touch and much more effective than in the past. We set over a decade-long record for creating new jobs in Oklahoma. The savings from these improved operations allowed us to spend more money on higher-priority areas. Two hundred million dollars was moved to education, a 30 percent increase, without raising taxes.

Not all of that credit goes to technology, but the technology set in motion an operating style that truly made a difference by transforming a slow, staid bureaucracy into a quick, responsible system. Many government people have become very excited about this change. They enjoy what they are able to accomplish over these systems, and they are much more effective than in the past. Let me share with you what I think is happening generally in the use of technology and telecommunications.

Many of the states have started passing "tax limitation laws." Our own state was the first to pass such a law, which says that without a vote we cannot raise taxes. But this of course puts a real damper on raising revenue to fund governmental services. Now, the public is demanding that government officials find ways to cut budgets and reallocate money. Telecommunications and technology allowed us to accomplish that much more effectively than we could in the past.

The technology also allowed us to decentralize services out into the field. We could create a single field office, for example, in which employment services, welfare applications, driver's licenses, and the like are all available to serve the public, while still communicating with the experts at their central offices. This breakthrough provides a form of one-stop shopping that many people only dreamt about government delivering. So I think the impact of this technology will allow the decentralization of government in a way that is far more responsive and efficient.

Some areas in the future that I am excited about involve the use of technology in welfare systems. If you go into the typical welfare office today, you will find rooms and rooms full of paper, telephones, and case workers who spend two days in the field visiting with clients but three days in the office filling out paperwork. Each of these case workers could be carrying a laptop computer, which they just plug in to their client's phone to transmit information back and forth. If they have a question or need to talk to someone, they can just get on their cellular phone. We can make these welfare officers more of a "virtual office" in which they can handle their enormous case loads far better by spending most of their work week in the field, reviewing cases and certifying them for welfare payments. The bottom line is, I believe we can save a sizable part of the welfare burden in this country. The potential savings are enormous when you consider the billions of dollars spent on welfare systems today.

Another important area is in our new telemedicine system. For a rural state this is a very exciting prospect, because our population is spread throughout the state where hospitals and physicians may not be available. We now have the largest computer-based telemedicine system in the country. By using this technology to put remotely located people in touch with health care services, we have been able to keep about twenty-five hospitals that were on the verge of financial collapse open in rural areas. Now, telecommunications allows us to transmit radiology results, blood tests, EKGs, and other medical data from patients located in small hospital facilities, rather than moving people to large and more expensive comprehensive hospitals. It's also far more convenient for the patients.

So telemedicine in our state is going to make an enormous difference in the quality of life of the people in our rural areas and small communities. We were pleased to be told recently by the rating agencies in New York City that Oklahoma is the first state to make medical information available electronically to them. That should help improve our bond ratings and lower the cost of our bonded indebtedness in the state.

Our constituents are seeking a variety of different services, and state government must take on a serious responsibility to serve these constituents better if we hope to carry out our mission to the satisfaction of the public. These responsibilities are growing more acute because we must not only provide effective services to various clients, we must do so in a far more efficient manner to serve the taxpayers who pay the bill. They have the political power to change the system.

One of the benefits from our use of technology is considered to be fairly creative, if not a little controversial. Although governments perform better if agencies work hard and save money, we have traditionally just taken the saved funds away from them at the end of the year by reducing their budgets. This is probably the craziest thing governments do, both at the federal and state levels, because it acts as a disincentive. The only result is that employees become tired and discouraged.

We began allowing agencies to keep their savings. Now, the trick here is that they may not get much additional money, but if they do a good job of organizing their operations, use their staff creatively, and apply sound management methods, they are permitted to keep any money they save.

This has been very beneficial to the state of Oklahoma. Our purchases in the last quarter of the 1993 fiscal year dropped something like a hundred million dollars for furniture and equipment. This shows that our employees have just avoided large purchases and made do with existing assets rather than give up their budgets. It's human nature.

Other savings were used to give employees a raise. Our state had too many employees by almost any measure in comparison with national averages. So we told agencies that if they could reduce their personnel budget through the sound use of technology and better management, they could use the savings for raises. Sure enough, the employees would usually get together and find a way to give themselves a raise. One national magazine called this practice the "Oklahoma carrot."

Not every agency was able to do that, but the majority of them did. Some say these differences are unfair, but I think that is the main point. This is the only way we are going to motivate agencies to make dramatic change. These policies, coupled with the use of telecommunications and technology, caused great excitement. Employees felt that they were in control of their own destiny, and therefore it has been generally accepted.

## Facing the Challenge

The costs of implementing such changes is not particularly high compared to what we spend on running today's bureaucracy. But this is not an easy task. There is enormous resistance among the agencies, within the legislative branches at times, and certainly among other vested interests that are worried about losing their grip over various aspects of the telecommunications industry. Independent telephone companies, for example, may or may not be happy with changes that you propose in state telecommunications systems because they have monopolies in certain parts of this business.

I found that a serious investment in training can help overcome much of this resistance. We have a very active vocational system in Oklahoma. It is separate and apart from the higher-education and elementary-secondary systems, with twenty-nine campuses around the state that are very modern and very well equipped. We funded a number of educational programs for agency managers and agency employees through this system. We also complemented the vocational education with total quality management. Roughly 60 percent of our employees went through that process. We also considered designating one of our universities in the state as a state employee training center and making it a quality management center.

Some of the benefits go beyond saving taxpayer money and providing better service. For instance, our electronic communication system proved absolutely essential after the bombing of the Federal Center in Oklahoma City in 1995. A crisis of this magnitude requires the help of countless federal, state, and local agencies, as well as a great many volunteer groups. The media alone sent in thousands of reporters from all over the world. Coordinating the efforts of these diverse groups in an emergency situation when ordinary communication systems are either down or severely limited is an enormous challenge. Fortunately, our e-mail, groupware, and Internet capabilities were available and proved up to the challenge.

I want to encourage other governments and institutions to re-vitalize their operations in the same way by using the powerful new information technologies that are rapidly becoming feasible for these purposes. It may require taking big risks, and you are often going to run into conflict, so sometimes you may fail. But more often than not, you are going to succeed. The creative use of tele-communications and computer technology can allow all of us to provide better governmental services at a much lower cost than we have in the past.

# 13

# Welcome to the Revolution

## Michael Malone

Welcome to the revolution. Why we are lucky to have it occur during our lifetimes is hard to say. The thing I find so astonishing is that we are able to assimilate all these radical changes fairly quickly. When Bill Davidson and I were writing *The Virtual Corporation*, we really debated whether to use the word "virtual." Nobody had ever heard of it, and so we were afraid it was too exotic a term. Now, everything is virtual. The virtual organization, the virtual office, the virtual community. I think this illustrates that we can adapt to this hectic pace of change.

### No End in Sight

That's the good news. The bad news is that it's not over. Look back over the past few decades of technological progress: the first computer operating on vacuum tubes was invented in 1945, the transistor in 1947, the microcircuit in 1959, the microprocessor in 1970,

---

Michael Malone is coauthor of *The Virtual Corporation* (New York: Harper Business, 1992) and the author of *The Microprocessor: A Biography* (Santa Clara, Calif.: Telos, 1995). He is a regular contributor to the *San Jose Mercury-News*, *New York Times*, and *Forbes*, and hosts his own show on PBS stations across the nation.

the PC in 1978, and so on. From that humble beginning of the Information Revolution, technological change has progressed through thirty-two orders of magnitude in terms of power, speed, cost, and size.[1]

That's an increase of ten followed by thirty-two zeros. It is estimated that the world contains two hundred billion chips of various types today, and the number is increasing exponentially as these smart little machines find their way into credit cards, light bulbs, dog collars, and auto tires. By the year 2010, computer chip making alone will comprise a $1 trillion industry.

Nothing else in human experience has increased thirty-two orders of magnitude. If these were distances, they would have increased from something comparable to the size of atoms to the millions of light years measuring our galaxy, the Milky Way. That is what we have been through. We try to cope like crazy, but it is still a struggle to assimilate the impact of seven generations of computer systems we have seen during this period. Naturally, people wonder how much more of this we have to go through. Where does it stop?

The answer is that it does not stop. At least not in our lifetimes. If you look at the many technological obstacles blocking the advance of microelectronics today, it appears that there is going to be a solution for every single one. By 2010, we may no longer have integrated circuits but a silicon or gallium-arsenide cube sitting in a cryogenic bath in the bottom drawer of your desk. Whatever the solution, it's going to happen. A PC will soon operate at one gigahertz and have one billion transistors. It will be like having ten Cray supercomputers in your hand.

## Shock Waves of Change

How do we cope with all that? One way is to recall that humans have been through this several times before, and each time they managed to surmount the challenge. The long march of civilization has progressed through multiple technological revolutions. First you harness the horse, then you invent a steam engine, next you attach the engine to a factory, and suddenly you have a four-times increase in productivity—the Industrial Revolution.

In these revolutionary periods, technology hits like a rock falling in a pond; then the impact ripples outward as shock waves of change. The first thing it affects is goods and services. After that it begins to change the enterprises that produce those goods and services. And finally it begins to transform society and culture.

Look at the Renaissance. Suddenly, you have double-entry book-keeping, then the large organizations that form the beginning of today's modern corporation. Later, we begin to see a complete transformation of society as people move from the country into cities: rise of the nation state, modern art, dispersion of the nuclear family, new structures in all of our institutions, and so on. All this occurs with basically two orders of magnitude change in performance and technology.

Although we have as yet felt only thirty-two orders of magnitude of change, we are going to end up going through about seventy-five orders of magnitude of change. Some very interesting things are happening for the very first time in history. Instead of a single rock falling in the pond and sending out one series of shock waves, we are getting hit by one rock after another every few years. The 286 microprocessor, the 386, 486, the Pentium, the P6, P7, and it keeps going.

So what happens? Well, the first wave of change spreading out from these falling rocks is that products and services begin to converge as we develop machines that can be programmed, that learn to evolve and adapt to the needs of the user. Ordinary greeting cards now often contain a short message, prerecorded by the sender on a chip that contains more power than the Eniac. Car tires contain chips that announce deviations from your chosen pressure, balance, and tread wear. Your hotel's door lock has an electronic brain that turns off the lights five minutes after you leave your room. In a short

*the importance of a tech revolution* [handwritten margin note] time, machines like your PC will learn your work habits and special tastes, and adjust automatically to serve these personal needs. Thus, service and product merge together until they become the same thing. They are created in real time, altering the very nature of business.

Wave two is that organizations then must change to produce these new product-services. These exciting new products are a wonderful advance, but unfortunately, to make these things you can't get there from here. You can't produce this type of thing with the traditional organization. It's too slow, has too many layers of hierarchy, with bureaucracy in between, and every one playing post office, changing the message on the way up and on the way down. The traditional advantages that once made you successful now become a burden. Scale no longer confers advantages, variety becomes cheap so there is no enduring source of profit. So we had to create a new type of organization.

## The Virtual Organization

That is where the virtual corporation comes in. The idea is that every function in the corporation can be performed far more effectively, cheaply, and quickly almost anywhere in the world using the newfound powers conferred by the Information Revolution. This transforms everything, some aspects of business more than others. We are seeing this trend everywhere: manufacturing is becoming fully automated, sales forces are using telemarketing and wireless systems operating from the field, MIS is replacing middle managers, employees are working from their homes, and all the other buzzwords we hear about.

The result is a new type of organization. Virtual relationships operate up and down the channels of command; outward to suppliers, distributors, and retailers sharing information with EDI; and all the way to the customer.

Ah, the customer! Remember the customer? In this new model the customer is everything. The entire goal of the virtual organization is to serve the customer better so he or she will bond with the firm, making us very profitable over time. We can keep people happy from the cradle to the grave if we do it right.

You wonder if your company should be centralized or decentralized, whether it should join a web of joint ventures or stand alone? The answer is, "What does the customer want?" There is a new driving force in all of this, and it is not customer satisfaction. That was hard enough because we know how tough it can be to satisfy people. Now we are moving on, we are aiming to create customer ecstasy!

And if you hope to provide these sophisticated product-services to make customers ecstatic, then you have to know every single thing about them. That is how we are going to make them ecstatic about what we are giving them. And we have to make them ecstatic to keep them forever because that is the only way we are going to make any money off of them. Because if we don't, then our competitors will and hang on to them forever, and then the body of available customers will get smaller and smaller. We are left with a smaller and smaller group of unhappy people.

So we have to know everything about them. We have to work with them. We have to bond with them. We have to bring them into the process. They have to help us with product creation, product design, product manufacturing, and product service. We have to support them in all sorts of ways we have not even thought of yet. Marketing's new job is, "Let's go out and find more folks to sell to." There are a lot of people out there. Marketing must support this body of customers, grow it, and keep it for an extended period of time.

Well, how are you going to get to know these customers? If somebody came to my door and said "Hi! I'm from Big Blue, and we want to know everything about your life. We want to know your tastes, your desires, your biases, your perversions. We want to know every single thing about you so we can give you exactly what you want," this person better run very fast. He or she better be off my property before the Winchester gets loaded. I am not going to give this information to these people. Yet they have to get it to give me what I want.

This takes us to another key idea in the virtual organization—trust. Unprecedented levels of trust. Trust between the supplier and the customer, between the designer and the manufacturer, between the employee and management.

Look at what is going on inside the corporation. We're handing down responsibility to all of these newly empowered employees. So managers have to trust their people when they give them all that power to make decisions. And they, in turn, have to trust you at the top. Your new job, as you are no longer micromanaging, is to actually be a leader. CEOs and top managers often liked to call themselves leaders before. But now they really have to do it. They have got to become the visionary for the company, to figure out how to hold the company together when you have employees telecommuting, people working at home, working in your supplier's offices, out there with your retailers—employees scattered all over the place. You have to find a way to keep them together, you have to give them a common vision.

But most of all, someone has to be there at the top, to stand at the apex of the corporation, looking out over the horizon to make sure that there aren't any missiles coming in from over the pole. Because that is where they are going to come from—surprising new technologies.

So that is the virtual corporation. But I'm not sure the company is going to get as flat as many say for two reasons: first, some of those middle managers actually did things, and second, someone has got to write the product applications for workers, and that is the middle manager's new job. The senior managers are now the philosopher kings. They are the visionaries and the scouts, whereas the middle managers become application designers.

The notion of a company made of transient people strikes me as absurd. The reason is that if you are keeping customers for life, they are calling in every week. But if they have to talk to somebody new, these are not going to be happy customers. Somewhere in the company there must remain a stable core competency. The people who carry forward the company's culture. The people who are the experts at what they do, who interact with customers. These people have to form a nuclear company at the core. Now maybe this core is surrounded by a cloud of people who are coming and going, contractors and part-timers and the like. But somewhere in there is a company. There may be a small building. It may be a place where people just meet to socialize. But there has to remain some measure of real company in there. The company is not just going to disappear. The virtual organization is not going to be like movie producers or a carnival, made up of dispersed individuals who just come together occasionally. Companies are an entity in themselves. They won't go away.

So as we begin to create smart new products and new forms of organization, the question arises: How and why do we choose to do this? We do not choose it—it chooses us! Just as the small-town craftsman was overwhelmed by mass production, so too will most attempts to retain the traditional corporation simply be overwhelmed by these new, fast-moving, agile, knowledge-based virtual companies. They are dangerous to existing companies.

## The Last Ripple of Change

We have one more ripple out there. As we move to a critical mass of virtual corporations selling smart products and services, as more customers use these goods to change their lives, as more people are employed in this type of knowledge work, society itself starts to transform itself in interesting ways.

The dominant metaphors for the Renaissance were perspective and double-entry bookkeeping, and for the Industrial Revolution they were mass production and hierarchial organization. In the type of society that seems to be emerging around us today, the dominant metaphor is information technology, and this metaphor maps on to the products, to the corporation, and to our culture. The key features of information technology that map over are two things: mass customization and the client server.

The rise of new products and services with intellectual content and built-in microprocessors is beginning to bring back some of those personal, customized touches we have lost. Look at the standard newsletter going out today. We used to go to a printer and graphic designer, who would put together a beautiful design, and then do a large print run. Well, that all ended with desk-top publishing. Unfortunately, most of our newsletters now look like an explosion in a font factory because most people don't have the skill to produce a good work of art.

In 1876, people attending the World Expedition saw the very first example of mass production and thought, "This is great. We will soon have harvesters, locomotives, and other ripples spreading out from mass production." The idea that we live in a society defined by mass production is completely pervasive. Customization is a rare exception. Right now people are looking at mass customization and saying this is nice, but only for Anderson windows, Luthron wall dimmers, and Motorola pagers.

But I would argue that mass customization will define every single aspect of the new society: all consumer products, including commodities. Because if you do not mass customize the products, you can mass customize the packaging, the delivery, and the like.

The second dominant metaphor is the client server, the new model of distributed computer processing and communications formed by a dispersed network of individual PCs that can operate together in a global system spanning the world. Our very lives are starting to gravitate toward these two dominant poles. At the technology level we are moving to the two extremes of the microprocessor versus telecommunications. In the corporation we are losing middle management, thereby creating the same polar opposites of the small, local, and individual versus the large, global, and universal.

In society, we are moving toward the grid, the Internet, the information superhighway, whatever you want to call it—that is one pole. But there exists a second pole that counterbalances the first, and we don't often talk about this enough. We are humans, and all those things that humans do will not disappear, they take on a new weight. We have to swap pheromones, to see the sweat on each other's brow. I would argue that just as technology and the corporation are moving to two poles, society will also move to these same two poles. If you are not at one of those two ends, you are in big trouble. If you are a regional government, or a regional corporation, you better start looking to choose which way to go. You will have already begun to see those tensions if you have looked out there.

So in this new society, we have two extremes of the local and the universal, mass customization and individual freedom within global information networks uniting the world. This poses a great challenge to all of us. We are about to address issues that stump philosophers. With all this freedom and choice, we have to be able to construct our world on a real-time basis, day to day. Are we prepared for that job? As the world turns upside down, each of us is at the apex of a pyramid, forced to find out what kind of a world we want to live in.

For some of us, it is going to be a wonderful, noble, lively experience because we can sit on top of Kilimanjaro and watch opera if we so choose. On the other hand, it will become an incredibly narrowing process as individualism grows rampant. The idea that we are going to hold hands in one big lovely community strikes me as utopian. It's just as likely that we will form a United States of 295 million small, personal nation-states. Each of us may just sit there and watch "I Love Lucy" reruns twenty-four hours a day on our virtual network because we are not prepared for anything else.

Everything is a two-edged sword. If you think about it, everything comes down to trust and the quality of education. I met a Renaissance scholar in Stockholm who told me, "Perhaps instead of teaching people skills we should go back to the Roman model and teach them three things: rhetoric, calligraphy, and dancing." It sounds a little silly, but if you think about it, that may prepare us more for this shifting, protean society of the future than anything else we are doing now.

## Note

1. For details, see Michael Malone, "Chips Triumphant," *Forbes ASAP* (Feb. 26, 1996).

*Steps to be an Create an Intelligent Org.*

*free intraprise w/ sense of community*

# 14

# The Intelligent Organization

## Gifford and Elizabeth Pinchot

As we enter the Information Age, the level of complexity that the Industrial Revolution brought to entire nations now exists in almost every mid-sized or larger workplace. Those organizations that deal intelligently with complexities and constantly changing environments do so by providing their people with extensive freedom of choice in how they do their work. This freedom includes what has been considered unthinkably inefficient: real choice between alternative vendors and partners within the organization as well as without. This right to choice we take for granted in nations with marketplace economies, just as the absence of that right, monopoly, has been the standard in centralized national economies.

The best alternative to an economy of nationalized businesses run by an authoritarian bureaucratic government is not a redesigned bureaucracy; it is a national economy largely directed by the intelligent choices of free people, both as individual citizens and members of organizations. As we all know, that doesn't mean anarchy;

---

Gifford and Elizabeth Pinchot are a husband-and-wife team who study, publish, and consult on progressive practices in organization and management. Their book *Intrapreneuring* (New York: Harper & Row, 1985) was a best-seller that introduced managers around the world to the need for entrepreneurship within corporations and other organizations.

what works is a system in which free citizens have rights and fulfill responsibilities. Their intelligent choices are guided by a combination of forces including marketplace exchanges, the spirit of community, and a limited government that focuses on establishing and regulating a set of institutions that make freedom work.

Now we are learning that systems structured to maximize self-organization are not only vital for healthy national societies and economies, but also for business firms, not-for-profits, and government agencies. Bureaucracy is no more appropriate to the Information Age than feudalism was to the Industrial Revolution.

The intelligent organizations of the future will be structured as networks of many smaller interacting internal enterprises (or *intraprises*). These organizational networks will be more reflective of markets and community structures of a free nation than the centralized administrative economy of a totalitarian nation. Intelligent organizations will be pluralistic to the core, preferring conflict between competing points of view and the struggle of competing internal and external suppliers to the illusory security of bureaucratic command and internal monopolies of function. The power to make fundamental work decisions—such as what to do and whom to do it with—will continue to be divested by the hierarchy and gradually distributed to smaller, self-managing intrapreneurial groups who make those decisions together. These small intraprises can be relatively independent of the hierarchy because what they deliver is accurately measured by the willingness of either internal or external customers to buy.

## Organizational Intelligence and Organizational Learning

Perhaps the greatest single advantage of organizations based on intrapreneurial networks is their ability to learn. Without the hindrance of bureaucracy, networks of intraprises create a precise and flexible order for serving customers cost-effectively. Within the guidance system of the firm's values and mission, intraprises are directed by the feedback received in the internal marketplace rather than by top-down design.

The intelligent organization continually reinvents itself by finding new ways to connect the intrapreneurial pieces. Forming new relationships that work (and losing those relationships that don't) is at the heart of organizational learning—learning to use the many talents and capabilities of the people in new ways. It is reminiscent of the way the brain learns by forming new synapses and keeping those that work while losing those that don't. A network that evolves from informed choices is the distinguishing characteristic of intelligent workplace communities.

## Increasing Freedom of Intraprise in Large Organizations

A debate rages between proponents of the efficiency of centralized service and those who believe that decentralization of functions will create greater responsiveness to divisional needs. But these two solutions are merely alternative flavors of bureaucracy and miss the larger point. The critical issue in organizational design is not centralization versus decentralization but monopoly versus choice (see Figure 14.1).

Neither of the organizational types in Figure 14.1 uses the discipline of user choice; their proponents are arguing over who should own the monopoly. Decentralization empowers the barons but, like the Magna Carta, it does little to empower the serfs. In either case, dissatisfied users have no recourse but to complain. Should they do so, the staff group is more likely to punish them than to respond with better service. Monopoly tends to complacency and indifference to customers' needs. What then is the alternative to internal monopolies?

One suggested antidote to bureaucracy is outsourcing (see Figure 14.2). James Brian Quinn points out that most work in a

**Figure 14.1. Centralized Staff Monopoly (Top)
Versus Decentralized Staff Monopolies (Bottom)**

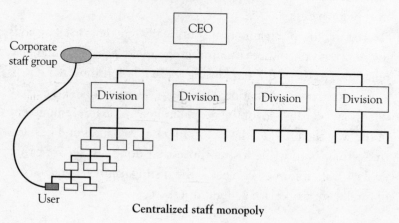

Centralized staff monopoly

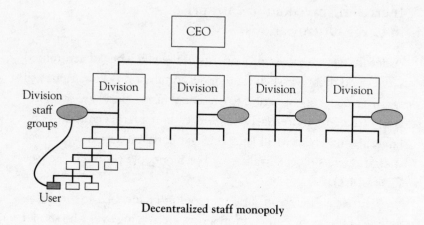

Decentralized staff monopoly

large organization consists of providing a service to another part of the organization. Whether the service provided is market research, maintenance, engineering design, or clerical work, all of these services can be defined, bought, and sold on the open market as readily as supplied by a staff group. For Quinn this suggests outsourcing most of the activities of the organization.[1]

The biggest advantage of outsourcing is that it restores the right to choose between responsive vendors—external, of course—rather than face internal providers, who hold a monopoly. Yet it may be

## Figure 14.2. Outsourcing: The Virtual Organization

**The Virtual Organization**

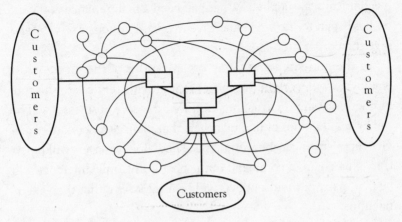

preferable to eliminate monopoly by encouraging the development of alternative suppliers and service providers within the organization. We see improved customer focus and quality of offerings when there are internal competitors to choose between—and without the disadvantages of outsourcing, which can include eliminating critical core competencies and reducing opportunities for new revenue. Let us give an example of the benefits of developing a competitive internal service provider.

The management of Union Carbide's Texas City plant established a Maintenance Shop Renewal Plan to tap the intrapreneurial spirit of its employees. It encouraged maintenance personnel to run their areas as if they were independent entrepreneurs. They could set their own prices, market their services, and bid for jobs against outside contractors.

Intrapreneur Bobbie Dillard saw the opportunity under the new plan to get more business for the machine shop and extend the savings to other plants. The machine-shop team he headed learned that it could recondition the seals in the plant's approximately 2,200 pumps for less than half the cost of rebuilding them at the factory, a savings of $200,000 in 1992. It then bid on the overhaul of two hundred seal parts at the nearby Taft, Louisiana, plant. The cost was less than a quarter of what Taft normally would have paid to its mechanical seal supplier.[2] What had been a maintenance cost center has begun to show revenue, give excellent customer service, and save the corporation money.

In the mid-sized and larger organizations of the future, most employees will work in intraprises that provide services to the core businesses. As in a virtual organization, the core businesses will be run by small groups of line managers that manage a network of service suppliers to get the work done. These line managers will report through a chain of command to the board. The only difference will be that many of their suppliers will be intraprises rather than external firms.

## Free Intraprise at DuPont

Early in the era of AIDS, the New York Blood Bank asked DuPont's Medical Products Department for help in tracking the history of every pint of blood passing through its hands. It needed a massive new database system right away, but although this DuPont department was its supplier, the department sold blood chemistry analyzers, not computer software.

Because the blood bank was a good customer, the Medical Products people sought help from their associated technology staffs. But these could not deliver the system within the ninety-day window demanded by the customer.

According to the rules of bureaucracy, Medical Products' people had done all they could for the customer. But they were too intrapreneurial and caring to give up that easily. They had heard of a small information technology group within DuPont's huge fibers business that was experimenting with a new system that could provide the needed software.

Of course, the Fibers Department had nothing to do with supplying medical customers or selling software. It made fibers for textiles, carpets, and industrial uses. But its small software group IEA (information engineers associates) had previously solved a problem very similar to that of the New York Blood Bank.

By the rules of bureaucracy, a staff group from one division is not supposed to do major jobs for other divisions. But this was an emergency, so IEA got the job. It delivered the blood-tracking database within the ninety-day deadline, far exceeding a major customer's expectations. Figure 14.3 shows IEA's place on the corporation's organization chart and indicates how it reached beyond the bureaucracy to achieve this end. Breaking bureaucracy's insistence on internal monopolies saved lives!

As IEA's reputation spread throughout DuPont, it found itself creating a database to track radiation in test wells around DuPont's nuclear materials production site at Savannah River. When it succeeded again in ninety days, the word spread and groups all over DuPont wanted its services.

Soon IEA's success became a problem: the Fibers Department had been paying its employees' salaries even as other departments used their services. At first, because Fibers managers were good corporate citizens, this was okay, but when IEA grew to fifty people

**Figure 14.3. IEA as a Third Choice for Information Technology**

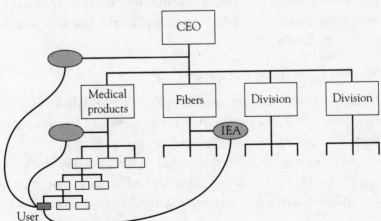

serving other departments they asked these people to do less work for other departments and focus on Fibers' needs.

IEA went to corporate finance for help, saying, "We don't want to be a staff group anymore. We want to be a profit center and live on what we can sell internally." The finance officer put on a glum face and said, "You are a staff function—you can't be a profit center." But then he winked, laughed, and said, "How would you like to be a 'negative cost center'?"

Soon the IEA intraprise had clients all over DuPont. Its revenues exceeded its costs, and so it grew to 120 employees. As the result of one leader creating the systems to support free intraprise exchange, business units all over DuPont began getting better information technology service at a lower cost.

In this story we see the beginnings of organizational intelligence. The growth of IEA was not ordered by the hierarchy; rather, it was mandated by the free-market decisions of customers. The new technology went where it was needed, not where some committee decided.

## The Institutions of Free Intraprise

Free internal markets can drive innovation, cost reduction, service quality, and customer focus. But it doesn't just happen. Free intraprise depends on a host of institutions. Many early efforts at freeing internal markets failed to put in place the necessary institutions to make it work.

### Systems for Forming Intraprises

If the basic right that creates free markets is the right to form an enterprise within the nation, that same right can allow a group of employees to form an intraprise within the organization.

An intraprise is a business unit still legally owned by the larger organization but operated and controlled internally by one or more intrapreneurs. In a free intraprise system, a team of people who believe they can do something better are free to set up an intraprise and serve customers in other parts of the organization. This concept offers a powerful force for the liberation of energy and intelligence of ordinary employees.

### Rights of Intraownership

Intraownership is an institution that grants something like property rights to intrapreneurs. Ownership is the right to control and dispose of something. Free-intraprise organizations grant a limited form of ownership to their intrapreneurs. Intrapreneurs have the right to control certain assets, such as tools, the intraprises themselves, and the earnings of the intraprises so long as they use them for the good of the organization.

In totalitarian states all property belongs to the state. Citizens may use things, but they can be taken away at any time by those above them in the chain of command. This greatly limits innovation and investment in the future. For example, in China, productivity gains in agriculture have almost ground to a halt because representatives from the collective reallocate plots of land every few years. Why would a family invest in terracing the land or building better irrigation systems when the benefit will most likely go to the next tenant? If ownership is shaky, only projects with very short payback will be undertaken.

Without private ownership it is hard to implement free enterprise in nations. Likewise, without something akin to ownership it is hard to implement free intraprise in workplaces. It is becoming traditional for employees to take their personal computer and the software on their hard drives with them when moving to a new office at the same company. Though legally still owned by the organization, the computer "belongs" to the employee in some real sense as long as he or she remains an employee. This informal ownership is the beginning of what we call *intraownership*—a kind of ownership that has power only inside the organization.

The rules that establish the institution of intraownership include the following:

- Intraproperty may be owned by individuals or intraprises. The intraowner controls the asset until he or she transfers ownership to another individual or intraprise or leaves the organization. In the case of leaving, intraownership may revert to the corporation or perhaps may be willed to someone else.

- Joint ownership of an asset is accomplished through shares. In the eyes of the outside world, intraproperty still belongs to the larger organization.

- The intraowner can use the intraproperty for any legitimate purpose of the organization, but not to break the law or to defy policy.

- The intraowner may or may not be constrained from using the intraproperty for personal pleasure or personal gain (for example, using an intraowned personal computer to moonlight).

- Ownership of intraprises and intraprise assets cannot be set aside without due process.

## Intracapital: A Medium of Exchange

After the idea of private property, perhaps the most liberating of economic institutions is the institution of money. One cannot fully appreciate what a liberating influence the existence of an agreed-upon medium of exchange is until one sees what people have to do in societies with an ineffective medium of exchange.

In our visits to the Soviet Union shortly before its collapse we became familiar with ways of doing business based on the exchange of favors rather than a standard medium of exchange. Transactions that in a market economy would have been negotiated directly between two parties in a few hours instead took several months and involved dozens of intermediaries. Though this sounds strange and inefficient, our experience in centralized corporate economies is similar. Getting resources for a project may take months of negotiation and the time and energy of dozens of managers. The solution to these problems requires an effective internal medium of exchange with which to buy and sell. We call such a medium of exchange *intramoney*.

In a free-intraprise organization, within the limits of their spending power units may buy and sell from one another by mutual consent. If, for example, I need some electron microscope pictures to analyze a product I am hoping to introduce, I get help from an electron micrographer in another part of the organization with whom I have had no previous dealings. I ask for several hours of work and offer $400 in intramoney as payment. The electron micrographer can add that intramoney to her intraprise account. She can spend it for an upgrade of her electron microscope, save it for repair services when the microscope goes down, or buy a training course. The added freedom that intramoney provides gives her a good reason to work hard to fit my pictures into her schedule. Without some low-friction medium of exchange for internal transactions, there can be no free intraprise worthy of the name.

### The Intracapital Bank

A sensible first step in creating the institutions of intramoney and intracapital is the establishment of a headquarters-sponsored intracapital bank. In the beginning it defines and establishes intramoney by being the place where intraprises (and individuals) may keep their intramoney and the bank on which they write intramoney checks. It creates a low-friction medium of exchange for internal transactions. Furthermore, having all internal transactions on the bank's computer makes calculating intraprise profitability quick and easy and provides a measure of control.

## Intracapital as Reward

We originally came up with the concept of intracapital to deal with
the challenge of rewarding intrapreneurial achievements. Let us
suppose a team does something wonderful for the organization and
we wish to reward its members. Perhaps it created $50 million in
new profits or got five thousand people off welfare and into productive jobs. If we give them a bonus of $1 million to share, all their
coworkers will be envious. Some will quit to start a business of their
own. If instead we give them $1 million to spend on behalf of the
organization, they are rewarded by being empowered to act freely
within the organization. This gives them a good reason to stay and
thus benefits their coworkers.

Intracapital is the reward that works twice. Not only is it an effective reward, but it puts funds in the hands of the most pragmatically
creative people in the organization—the proven innovators.

*I disagree, they need some compensation* [handwritten marginal note]

## Intracapitalism as Empowerment

The institution of free enterprise would be far more limited if the
only source of capital for entrepreneurs were their own savings.
Entrepreneurs capitalize their projects with other people's money.
Similarly, a full-blown free-intraprise system needs effective institutions for intracapitalism—allowing successful intrapreneurs to invest
their excess intracapital in intraprises that are just starting out.

## Relationships of Productive Interdependence and Freedom

The free intraprise system is free because the system is flexible and
filled with choice for everyone involved. Individuals and teams can
choose what to contribute and how to structure their work as long
as they deliver enough value to customers to cover their costs. Each
individual is free to form an intraprise of his or her own or to join
in one or more intraprises with others. All those choices create an
ever-changing intricate network structure—a structure constantly
adjusted as though an invisible hand were guiding everyone to find

the best use for their talents. For all its freedom, free intraprise produces a powerful customer focus no bureaucracy can begin to match.

## The Power of Community

Although there is growing attention to the hunger for community, there is scant appreciation of community as a powerful force for order in human systems. Community is a full partner to the free internal marketplace in bringing order and cooperation to the intelligent organization.

### Community in the Windows NT Development Project

When David Cutler began managing the development of Windows NT, the computers his programmers used were running O/S2 (an IBM system that competes with Windows). But one day, as the new operating system developed, Cutler said, "We will let the dogs eat their own dog food." He proclaimed that the Windows NT programmers were to take O/S2 off their computers and instead use the embryonic system they were developing. Having to struggle with all the bugs and inconveniences of the half-finished Windows NT raised the urgency of making it work. It also brought the powerful force of community strongly into play.

There were about 250 programmers in teams of five to fifteen working on NT. Each week (and eventually each day) the work of all the teams was integrated into the existing system. If you were part of a team that fixed a major bug or inconvenience, you did not need David Cutler to tell you you were hot stuff. The glances you got on the way to the water cooler told a tale of rising status. But if your team's code crashed everyone's computers, dehydration might set in as you hid from your peers. Again, there was no need for Cutler to provide feedback and control.

Following the logic of community, which is hard-wired into the human psyche, the programmers strove to raise themselves in the eyes of their peers by making contributions to the usability and robustness of the system that was their common environment. Irrespective of the hierarchy, everyone wanted to contribute. No one wanted to let the group down.

David Cutler applied one of the great principles of Information Age system design: he increased the force of community by making the contributions (and shortcomings) of his people more visible. By doing so, he placed them in the mind space of the gift economy.

## The Gift Economy

In his brilliant book *The Gift: The Erotic Life of Property*, Lewis Hyde describes two types of economic systems. In what he calls a commodity (or exchange) economy, status is accorded to those who have the most. In a gift economy, status is given to those who give the most to others.

In the potlatches of the Chinook, Nootka, and other Pacific Northwest peoples, the chiefs vied with each other to give the most valuable gifts. More generally, in hunter-gatherer societies the hunter's status in the community is not determined by how much he keeps for himself, but rather by what he brings back for others.

Lest we think that the principles of a gift economy only apply to "primitive" peoples, consider the world of science. At a symposium a scientist *gives* a paper. The scientists with the most status are not those who possess the most knowledge, they are the ones who have contributed the most to their fields. A scientist with great knowledge but only minor contributions is almost pitied. A forgetful scientist who knows little but somehow each year produces breakthroughs is revered. Science, the world's first Information Age industry, more closely follows the rules of the gift economy than the rules of exchange.

The rules of the gift economy are the rules of community. When we are in community we are intrinsically motivated to contribute and are well regarded to the degree to which we do. Moment by moment, most people at work are motivated more by a desire to be seen as a good contributor than they are by thinking about their next promotion. Whether we work hard or not, it often seems our salary will be the same. Yet in many cases, even when the boss will never know what we did, we take great satisfaction in a job well done. When someone asks for a bit of information, we give it expecting nothing in return but respect, for we respect those to whom everyone goes for help. Day-to-day work inside a large organization, like the enterprise of science, apparently follows the rules of community and the gift economy.

Without a functioning community no organization, town, or nation can escape from descent into the mean-spirited barbarism of "everyone for oneself." Free enterprise may be a good way to organize the businesses of the town, but without voluntary contributions to the churches and cultural institutions it would be a sad place to live. Without community spirit, the free market would not enjoy the reputation it has today.

Within our workplaces, free intraprise creates a base of liberated corporate citizens who can make choices without fear. It is an ideal base for an organizational community based on voluntary contributions rather than fear of hierarchy. But without a powerful organizational community, free intraprise, no less than hierarchy, will fail to bring out the best its people have to offer.

How, then, can we create organizational community?

## A Worthwhile Vision

One of the fundamental tasks of leadership is to lift people out of selfish and parochial concerns and inspire them to work together toward the good of the whole. Worthwhile visions bring out community spirit.

The best visions stretch the organization beyond what is obviously achievable, thereby creating the necessity for innovation. AT&T's old rallying cry, "universal service," provided guidance to everyone from the serviceman climbing the pole in a storm at 4 A.M. to the negotiator getting the Public Utility Commission to agree to rates high enough to provide funds for running a line four miles out to the desolate ranch run by a widow, who needed the phone for emergencies. It even inspired the engineer to provide a faster and more reliable dial tone. Everyone was inspired in their work by striving to provide universal service. This was part of how AT&T became a community, not just a company.

The best way to create inspiring meaning is to involve as many people as possible in creating the vision. Great leaders detect the greatness hidden in the mind of the people and give it voice.

### A Bias Toward Equality and Diversity

Symbols of status like executive dining rooms and special parking places for big shots are very destructive of community spirit. Both in Japan and Silicon Valley, the best companies have discovered the advantage of eliminating everything (from different uniforms to separate rest rooms) that makes the ordinary corporate citizen feel small. In the best organizations everyone, regardless or race, sex, age, job, or talent feels they have full membership in the community.

### The Information Freedoms

Employees won't feel part of a community nor can they make responsible choices if they don't know what's going on. Bureaucrats tend to hoard information as a source of personal power. The intelligent organization creates a rich bath of what Max DuPree of Herman Miller calls "lavish communication."

These are the minimum requirements:

- Full financial information for all employees and training in how to read financial statements

- Regularly posted measurements for all activities

- Open discussion of strategic options and competitive situations

- Frequent discussion of how each part fits with the whole

- Freedom of internal speech

- Freedom of internal Web site postings and e-mail

- Right of inquiry and learning in order to pursue the mission and best serve customers and the organization

### Internal Not-For-Profits

Worthwhile projects inside a corporation are sometimes funded through "tin-cupping"—getting a number of business units to contribute to a project of general usefulness. We also find formal and informal associations whose purpose is the exchange of information. In advanced intelligent organizations, these manifestations of internal community will be supported by the institution of internal not-for-profits. They will have charge numbers, bank accounts, and all the accoutrements of formal reality. This will help to put the tasks of community on a formal, self-organizing basis suitable to the complexity of the Information Age.

### Limited Governance from Above

For all its virtues, the free market doesn't always produce a good solution. Nor does community spirit answer all the remaining challenges. Consider, for example, fraud, extortion, and pollution. Effective market systems rightly limit the freedom of firms to dump dangerous chemicals or to compel customers to "buy" protection with threats of bodily harm.

Internal "laws" are needed when actions repeatedly benefit the part at the expense of the whole. Justice and a body of internal law create the context in which the many actions of enterprising individuals and teams lead to a coherent order and productive outcomes.

Rather than depending on bureaucratic supervision to prevent abuses, intelligent organizations grant freedom limited by clearly stated laws and an effective justice system. The result: both more freedom for innovation and better control.

## Establishing the Institutions of Free Intraprise

The institutions of free intraprise will not arise by themselves. In the face of bureaucracy's powerful tendency to remove freedoms, free institutions are created and defended by the central government of an intelligent organization. These include the right to form an intraprise, intraownership, the intracapital bank, the appropriate accounting systems, and so forth.

### Right to Make and Honor Commitments

Many productive relationships involve more than an instantaneous trade. They involve the making and keeping of longer-term commitments. In most bureaucracies, no one other than officers or perhaps even the board has the formal right to make a binding promise to another employee. All promises made about such things as who will work on a project or what resources will be available can be set aside by those above in the chain of command. This lack of predictable agreements greatly decreases long-term thinking, innovation, organizational learning, efficiency, and morale.

Typically, effective managers get around the fact that they are not empowered to make contracts by making informal promises that they then strive mightily to keep. But it is not always easy to do this when the system does not value the integrity of its members enough to allow them to keep their commitments. For example, the vice president of operations for a regional U.S. railroad offered his engineering officers a deal. Because there were cycles in the availability of capital to maintain the plant and equipment, the managers feared there might be a capital freeze just when they needed to replace track or rolling stock. As a result, they routinely replaced equipment well before the end of its useful life.

"Don't put in for major repairs to the plant or equipment years before they are needed," he begged. "Instead, put them off until the year when they actually should be done, and I will personally guarantee that they will be approved that year."

Several of the officers reporting to him made great savings for several years. Finally, they came to the end of the safe lifetime of several sections of rail. However, at that time there was a corporate capital spending freeze. Although the vice president shook the system with all the power he had, he could not get their requests approved. The result was a number of derailments. No one involved escaped with their sense of integrity intact. The vice president quit. The engineering managers felt personally responsible for the derailments. They went back to padding their requests and playing the wasting game that goes on in every bureaucratic budgeting process.

The government of an intelligent organization creates the internal systems for recording and enforcing contracts between members of the organization, including managers, business units, ordinary employees, intrapreneurs, and intraprises.

## A System of Justice

The society without justice becomes not only mean, but also short-sighted. We have seen these tendencies in many corporations, government agencies, and not-for-profits. The informal organization can handle the small and short-term agreements, but the longer-term and larger-scale forms of cooperation just fail to materialize.

The quality of an organization's system of justice can provide a significant competitive advantage. In our lives as citizens of nations, we have become inured to inefficient justice and bad policy and law. Our legislative and legal systems are held hostage to numerous special interest groups. Projects within our workplaces to develop more intelligent internal legal systems create a fresh opportunity for collaboration between political philosophers, pragmatic leaders, and members of the organization. A high-quality system of justice is swift, inexpensive, and fair. It provides great latitude for innovation and new ideas and at the same time moves swiftly to stamp out destructive behavior.

## Education

Fast-moving small intraprises, like the hard-pressed business units of today's bureaucracies, may find it difficult to take time and funds to educate their people. In most societies, support for education is a government and community responsibility. In the intelligent organization, supporting education remains one of the critical roles of the center. It is both part of the community support that keeps every member of the organization at its best, and an essential strategy for continued organizational competitiveness.

## Organizational Learning Resources

In a chain-of-command organization there is no dependable and liberating source of funds for the information synthesizers, archivers, editors, creators, brokers, illustrators, writers, and boundary crossers needed to create the organizational mind. Information, when it is passed on, is passed on "for the good of the whole." As downsizing removes spare time and resources, time for such "community service" is growing scarce. Though we can do much to increase the power of community spirit, community spirit alone is not enough to keep all the knowledge workers of the organization networking to create an organizational brain. *need I sources and freedom of those sources*

Free intraprise provides a far more powerful mechanism for funding and regulating information gathering, generation, storage, packaging, transfer, and evaluation that are at the core of organizational intelligence. In the external world, gathering and distributing information is a big business. We have magazines, books, journals, radio, television, movies, universities, schools, consulting firms, patents, and more. Free intraprise creates an organizational framework for selecting and funding a host of liberated knowledge intraprises. When coupled with Information Age rights such as free speech and freedom of the press and intraWeb, we create a framework for building and sustaining a self-aware and self-correcting organizational intelligence.

## Making and Breaking Connections

Like a free-enterprise nation, a free-intraprise organization is made up of a constantly shifting network of relationships. Relationships that add value are maintained. Relationships that deliver inadequate value are unprofitable and are dropped. This is a basic process of organizational learning, much like the formation and destruction of synapses in the brain.

An interesting analogy: after age six the number of synapses in the human brain is cut in half. It seems that the brain begins with all possible connections and learns by paring away those that are not useful. The person learns by disconnecting the unworkable relationships inside the brain.

Bureaucratically structured organizations are very slow to disconnect relationships that are not working. In fact, without choice and market feedback, they have no honest mechanism for evaluating the productivity of information pathways or the parts of an internal value creation web. Free intraprise organizations, however, can learn by trying new connections and using the feedback of the internal market to cut away what isn't cost effective.

The following list summarizes the steps to create an intelligent organization. The framework requires three institutional pillars: internal free enterprises, a limited central power, and a sense of community shared throughout the organization.

*Ten Steps to the Intelligent Organization*

1. Establish quick and easy systems for setting up intraprises, especially for those serving internal customers.

2. Establish institutions for defining and registering joint ownership of an intraprise.

3. Create an "intracapital bank" that allows every business unit and intraprise to function as if it had a bank account in which to deposit its receipts and to "write checks" to other internal units against the balance.

4. Create a strong, shared vision through widespread participation.

5. Create a strong corporate safety net to catch and support those who lose their jobs within an intraprise.

6. Promote internal contributions to common organizational causes. (Create the internal equivalent of not-for-profits.)

7. Establish company-wide profit sharing or worker ownership to increase cross-system cooperation.

8. Create a system for registering agreements and contracts. Make sure everyone treats promises, their own and those of others, with great respect.

9. Create a fast and efficient internal justice system with fair courts and judges to which disputes can be taken.

10. Create an effective process for rapidly establishing a body of internal "commercial law." Use the larger society's commercial law as a starting point, but seek simpler and faster procedures.

## Notes

1. James Brian Quinn, *Intelligent Enterprise* (New York: Free Press, 1992), p. 41.

2. "The Internal Entrepreneurs," *UC World Magazine* (Fall 1993), p. 5.

# 15

# An Advertising Agency Without Walls

## Robert Kuperman

Chiat/Day is a very successful twenty-five-year-old advertising agency that was started in Los Angeles and now employs seven hundred people. We have experienced double-digit growth during this time. In two instances we doubled our size as a result of major new accounts. These included Apple, for which we produced the famous "1984" commercial showing a young woman throwing a hammer at Big Brother. We also created the Energizer bunny ads, as well as others for Nike, Pizza Hut, and other large companies. We have been cited as Agency of the Year many times, and also as Agency of the Decade.

However, the history of advertising shows that no creative agency has remained dominant into its second generation of management. So we realized for some time that the challenge of continuing to thrive revolves around really understanding what we would have

---

Robert Kuperman is a founder of Chiat/Day Advertising Agency, one of the major firms in the business. The company is headquartered in Los Angeles and has operations around the world. In 1995, Chiat/Day merged with TBWA Advertising, a unit of the Omnicomm Group. Kuperman is a prominent member of the advertising community. He has received more than five hundred awards and is consistently cited as one of the top hundred advertising people in the United States.

to face in the future. With that goal in mind, our chairman, Jay Chiat, asked me to lead a group called the Chrysalis project. Our job was to examine trends in the advertising business, the coming needs of our clients, and the general environment of the future.

This study led to the transformation of Chiat/Day into the world's first "virtual advertising agency." It was one of the most ambitious early efforts to apply concepts of the virtual organization. The effort succeeded in redefining how companies are organized in our business, and it forced all of us to reconsider our basic assumptions about how creative people can work best.

Not everyone responded the same, of course, but we generally came to see that the old idea of making a comfortable home in your office is not the same thing as being productive. In an era when information networks constantly carry our thoughts around the world at the speed of light, modern people are challenged to learn how to recreate that comfortable sense of belonging in their hearts and minds as they interact with others throughout a busy day. As Jay Chiat put it, "I thought it would be a big improvement if people stopped organizing their day around where they sit and instead focus on what they do."

## The Chrysalis Project

We spoke to a great number of people in business and academia. We looked at all industries and all sectors of society. Our main conclusions focused on three key points:

1. Unless a company has the ability to manage change faster than its competition, it will fail.

2. Modern companies need to use technology in a strategic manner and to transform information into intelligence quickly.

3. The fifty-year-old tradeoff on which American business was founded no longer held. We used to believe that you can have it good, you can have it fast, or you can have it cheap—please pick one. The Japanese proved this false by delivering all three.

We learned that to exist in the future, companies have to possess the strategic intelligence to deliver a product of high quality and extremely good value, and to do this very quickly. Any company that cannot is doomed to failure.

We became very concerned about adapting to change. It is essential to estimate what the future holds and to develop the ability to adjust continuously and instantaneously. The old approach of calming the organization down and getting people settled is no longer possible if you want to stay competitive.

For the advertising business, things are changing drastically. We are now dealing with a very savvy consumer who is well educated, tends to be distrustful, shows little brand loyalty—and has a very short attention span. We all know that people now hold the power of the TV remote control in their hands. Zapping commercials is a major new reality that every advertiser has to face.

In terms of media, the traditional way we delivered our messages has become highly fragmented. We use cable and we use the networks, but they are no longer the kind of mass communicator that they were in the past. For our clients the problem is just as complex. The idea that they could produce a product that would continue to be of benefit against the competition for any length of time has quickly faded. If they bring something great out, it is easily copied. So we are really dealing with a commodity market, products that gain parity at best.

What we felt we needed was an organization that had an adaptable core. We felt we needed to do everything we could to realize this vision. It had to be an organization that took its cues from nature, from life itself—one that is able to continually adopt to its environment, that picks up any change affecting its business and responds effectively and immediately.

The corporate philosophy that resulted is based on a continual examination of all stakeholders to better understand current operations and to improve our ability to explore future opportunities. We consider suppliers and distributors to be sources of recommendations for process improvement. Employees are viewed as the company's most important source of intelligence. Customers are regarded as long-term partners. Together, these groups form the heart of a teaching and learning dialog that is open and continual.

This is the organization we wanted to become. To achieve it, we needed to encourage experimentation, promote constructive dissent, acknowledge failures, and continue to move ahead.

Like most agencies we talked a lot about teamwork, but basically we were structured in the old departmental towers. The basic processes for ad agencies are account management, creative design, and media planning. Even though these people worked together, what it came down to at the end of the day is that they were responsible for their departments. They were primarily concerned about their own departmental goals instead of those of the agency as a whole.

What we had to do was break down this departmental structure. So we went to a dramatically different structure in which all needed functions were integrated into strategic business units (SBUs). Each of these units is a small team responsible for certain clients. The core of the team consists of the creative people, the media planner, the account manager, and the consumer research function. This team is supported by the service departments in the agency. The service departments are judged by how well they support these SBUs.

We form these units based on what the client needs, not on what the agency feels the structure of the SBU should be. Each member of that core team, regardless of his of her discipline, is responsible for the end product. Each SBU has its own profit and margin goals to make. They are given bonuses based on how they perform. We felt this was a major step to creating an organization that truly operates as a cooperative network of teams.

We soon found, however, that although we had changed the organizational structure we were still limited by our building's physical architecture. The building's traditional layout promoted an "office mentality"—it encouraged people to sit in individual spaces with individual knowledge. We realized that it was important to take a look at how we could push collaboration by constructing a new architecture that is conducive to teamwork. Basically, we said to ourselves, "If we are truly in the idea business, why does thinking only take place in our offices? Do creative ideas only arrive between 9 A.M. and 5 P.M.?"

The answer was clear. To really liberate people from the Industrial Age boundaries of an office, we did away with the personal office. In effect, we gutted the building.

## Transforming the Company

Chiat/Day was not a very hierarchical organization before these changes were made. We never had titles on our business cards. No one had offices with closed doors, but cubicles. So this was a rather open place, an organization that was pretty well adapted to change.

But even this fairly sophisticated organization had problems with the changes we finally made. The day the agency went virtual was high anxiety. The building, only two years old, was being reconstructed, so people were being uprooted once again. And instead of returning to their former desks and cubicles, they found only common areas, project rooms, and a small locker for their personal belongings.

Basically, we installed a completely different working architecture. The new plan centered around project rooms. Each of our standing clients or temporary projects were given a room where the members of their SBUs meet as a team. The rest of the organization consisted of support units that surround these project units. We like to think of this as a "university model" because people come to the office when they feel the need and can move freely about any of those areas. I will talk specifically about each of the issues this architecture imposed.

The first need we dealt with was communication. Every employee at Chiat/Day was assigned a "virtual extension number." It is a "phantom direct-dial line." Our common phone system responds to that system, whether I am working at home, a hotel, the client's office, in my car, or somewhere in between. My calls go through to reach me wherever I am, and the entire process is totally transparent to the caller. That is, they don't really know where I am, and they usually don't care as long as they get through to me. We also have located portable radio phones in all offices to allow people to move around the building. This is important so people can remain in contact wherever they happen to be.

The second great change was to create a computing system based on client-server architecture. This reduced the need for powerful individual computers, which were replaced by smart terminals that simply access the central system. The design of our computer system features collaboration among areas where information is shared. We no longer move information from person to person because this is a horrible waste of time. Rather, we post it in the system and have the computer notify the right people that a file or advertising copy has been posted.

As a result, our old giant manila sacks and huge mechanical files have been replaced by "electronic job jackets" containing all needed information and digitized photography. Legal reviews and proofreading comments are added electronically and relayed automatically to the central file. We do not have traffic managers running around with paper, faxes, and the rest. All key documents are the collective property of the agency, available to all who want or need to use them. You do not have to worry about whether you have the latest copy because it always exists in the computer.

All employees are assigned portable Power Books based on their needs. We have a combined worldwide e-mail system and also a remote access capability to allow anyone to access anything they need from anywhere in the world as long as they can get a dial tone. The library is plugged in to this network, providing the ability to pull up information from anywhere instantaneously. Documents can be scanned optically to enter new files electronically.

So we really possess the freedom to work anywhere we want, to accomplish what we need to do regardless of time and place. The idea is that you only have to come to the office as a matter of choice. Geography is no longer important. While in the building, people work while walking around together from one place or group to another, occasionally pressing a wireless phone to their ear or pausing to use one of the many "information fountains"—computerized work stations perched atop lecterns that allow one access to the computer system. I think our employees are now more creative and productive because they are treated as adults. They are assessed and rewarded on the basis of performance rather than on child-like rules regarding attendance.

## The Outcome

Results of going virtual took different forms. In terms of our use of physical space, the building now houses the same number of employees in one-third as much space. Eliminating the unneeded offices reduced our investment in real estate by $1.2 million.

The greatest impact was on the way people work. Laurie Coots, our senior vice president in charge of administration and business development, personally managed things through the turmoil of change. She estimates that about 20 percent of the staff were resistant to the concept, another 25 percent were excited by it, and the rest were in the middle, wondering how to adapt and how it would work.

Part of the staff was upset because losing their office meant a loss of their "emotional anchor," the place where they kept photos of their family, comfortable old chairs, and a private place to be alone—their ego. Some even shifted this need for personal space to their lockers. They equipped their lockers with files, photos, and PCs, making it possible to stand there and work out of the locker as if it were a small office.

But most saw the move as a gain in freedom. One manager went into a cleaning frenzy and threw out all the old stuff he had accumulated over years, filling seven garbage bags. "It was like going cold turkey," he said. "It felt great. I was suddenly liberated." Another claimed, "When we first switched, I had a hard time with my stress level. I couldn't go to my own little haven and put my feet up to think. Then I realized that it's not really your surroundings that make you comfortable, it's you. Now I can relax in the middle of a street." And one put it this way: "Now I feel like this whole place is my office. I can walk into any space on any floor and say, 'Let's hang something there,' and I can do it. I have the freedom to make the whole place mine."

Generally speaking, I think the goal of Jay Chiat has been realized. Jay put it this way: "The virtual office is not about working at home. It's about making the workplace a resource rather than a place where you have private storage bins with material that becomes obsolete. So instead of coming to the office and knowing where you're going to sit, now you have to come in and know what you're going to do."

The building now has a pace of activity and interaction that is electrifying at times. Chiat calls it an "idea factory" that gives off "raw energy" and "subconsciously demands that you do something a little unique." The "Club House" or "Student Union" is a large open space housing comfortable chairs, pool tables, espresso machines, a cluster of large TV monitors flashing news and entertainment, and an outdoor deck overlooking a snack bar with dining booths. In one corner lies a row of punching bags with the faces of Chiat executives on them for people to take out their aggression. Lee Clow, the agency's creative genius, calls it "the cocktail party model of work," and Laurie Coots says, "If you're one of those people who couldn't study in college unless the TV or radio was blaring, this is the place to go."

The biggest and most important impact is that people collaborate more effectively. Whether it's a small, quiet conversation in a sitting area or a large, intense meeting, the focus is now on results.

A team working on the Nissan account had to pull together a major presentation for the client in a few days. Here's how a member of the team described its work: "Normally, this would have taken us three days. Instead, we all gathered in the project room with our computers and our phones. All of our brains were working and our ideas flowing. We put the presentation together in two hours. I couldn't believe it. Okay, I thought, this is what it's all about." Laurie Coots reports that work does tend to happen in shorter and more intense bursts.

Financially, I don't think we could justify over the short term the investment in technology and training we had to make. We spent about $6 million on this project, and it did not balance out in the first year or two.

But the benefits began to be more striking over the long term. The agency saw big improvements in performance, especially in our responsiveness to clients. I would say that the change succeeded in creating a new form of organization that was better suited to serve our clients' unique needs with ease and speed. Some companies, such as Coca-Cola, simply want to meet with their account team briefly for discussion, while others, such as Nissan, expect their agency to get deeply involved in their business in order to fully understand how to approach their job better. Because clients differ in their needs, the advertising organization has to reconstruct its capabilities instantaneously around the client. It has to customize how its personnel interact with their people. That's what the virtual agency allowed us to do.

I also feel that it enhanced the brand name of Chiat/Day. Since going virtual, we have acquired $90 million in new business, producing net income of $9 million. This success encouraged us to expand the concept to our New York and Canadian offices.

But I must caution that this is not a one-time change effort; it is an ongoing process with no end, especially because management can't really control it. Management can support it and guide it to some extent, but not control it. We hold occasional meetings to air complaints and consider moving this effort in new directions, but basically the organization is now a thing with a life all its own. I find that the more control you try to exert, the more it starts to look exactly like the system you had before. If you let it design itself, if you open up, it starts to take off. You see people come to use their best possible abilities.

We're not quite there yet, believe me. Some people think we'll revert back to the old system if this doesn't work out. But I think we have got to make this succeed because the old way doesn't work anymore. There is no going back. We've left the past.

# 16

# Riding the Information Tiger

## William A. Owens

The wonderful thing about revolutions is that they unleash the power of the people caught up in them. The scary thing is that they unleash the power of the people caught up in them. Revolutions are one of those great paradoxes: a fragile balance of creation and destruction, hope and despair, gain and loss. They're what inspires some to write of "the best of times and the worst of times" and others to compare revolutions to . . . well, tigers: powerful, fast-moving, dangerous, beautiful bundles of energy that defy prediction. Of course, our business at SAIC is not to be poetic about the Information Revolution. We're in business to ride that particular tiger.

How do you ride the Information Revolution, metaphorically speaking? I think it boils down to building the type of organization and processes that fit the character of this particular revolution. So, taking Bill Halal's introductory description of the Information Revolution as a fast-moving, not-entirely-predictable phenomenon, it

---

William A. Owens is president, COO, and vice chairman of the board of Science Applications International Corporation (SAIC). He was previously commander of the U.S. Navy's Sixth Fleet, vice chairman of the Joint Chiefs of Staff, and senior military adviser to the Secretary of Defense. Owens is a graduate of the Naval Academy and received an MA degree from Oxford University and an MBA from George Washington University.

helps to have an organization that is flexible enough to cope with the unpredictability, and processes that are agile enough to respond quickly to the twists and turns.

To fit the speed and diversity of the Information Revolution, you need a lot of sensors out there, a wide range of perspectives and pursuits. I think you also need a particular view of the future that recognizes the human penchant for continuity *and* the speed at which things develop. The prevailing view of information technology, after all, is that things change, sometimes profoundly, every eighteen months. I remember a discussion with Bill Gates on long-range planning. As far as Gates was concerned, two years is as far out as long-range planning should go; anything beyond that is long-range dreaming. He suggested that technology is changing so rapidly that it is not only difficult to predict where it will be in a couple of years, but even dangerous to try. Corporate planning that goes beyond the next two years, in his view, acts as a constraint to opportunities that pop up.

So how do you build an agile company, with a lot of sensors, able to move quickly to exploit the speed and dynamism of the Information Revolution? Or, to use the terms spawned by this particular revolution, how do you create a company that allows teams to act as nodes in an information network that unites the organization, allows it to respond dynamically, and builds synergy among the parts? And an equally important issue: How do you do this without making those "nodes" feel like they are simply cogs in some great machine over which they have no influence?

Perhaps SAIC offers some answers: get the best people, and push decision making downward in a decentralized organization. That gives you the responsiveness, agility, and initiative to stay ahead of the Information Revolution. Then, tie the company together by giving its people a direct, material interest in the company's success, and add robust, innovative flows of information. That builds synergy and lets you harness the full strength of the company.

## People: Building Nodes, Not Cogs

SAIC was formed and operates on two broad principles. The first is to use the best people on important problems. The second is to give those people a personal stake in coming up with good solutions. It's worth a few lines about the inherent meaning and power of these foundation concepts.

Consider the first—the best people working to solve important problems. "Best" encompasses those attributes we associate with the kind of people everyone likes to work with: intelligence, tenacity, and honesty, for instance. On the second, how do you identify an "important" problem? One idea is that the relative importance of any issue almost always has to do with the number of people it affects. Also, the value of what is at stake—what may be gained or lost—is important. Put these two concepts together and you've got a pretty good standard of importance. Important problems affect a lot of people in high-value areas. That's why SAIC focuses its effort on national security, energy, and health care problems.

The best people working on important problems doesn't necessarily guarantee the best solutions to those problems. A lot depends on how you organize the effort.

## Decentralized Organization

We work within a very flat organization. The core of SAIC is composed of a corporate headquarters and forty-two separate profit centers, each with considerable autonomy over their budgets, plans, personnel, and business decisions. It is an organization that expects and enables an entrepreneurial approach toward problem solving throughout the corporation. It is an organization that facilitates quick and flexible responses by placing decision authority for resource allocation in the hands of those in direct contact with their customers.

The customer does not have to wait for an answer on a given project until someone in corporate headquarters has received the question, assessed it, asked for clarification, canvassed other affected offices, assembled the necessary opinions and data, made a decision, and passed that decision back down to the operating group. We expect groups to make decisions and to provide their clients with fast, accurate responses. And they do.

## Employee Ownership

Okay, so we've got the best people working on important problems in a decentralized structure. Some important centrifugal forces figure in this. Good people can find jobs just about anywhere, and important problems are always going to be "growth areas" looking for good people. Also, decentralization can contribute to fragmentation and spin-offs. So what holds it together?

Let's look at the other SAIC foundation principle—employee ownership. Employee ownership is the most direct and the best means of capitalizing, literally, on SAIC's assets. When the current chairman of the board and CEO, Dr. J. Robert Beyster, founded the company over a quarter century ago, he began the endeavor with the view that SAIC would focus on long-term growth. Beyster and his original team of scientists were after a stable research and development environment in which highly talented individuals would focus on creative research. But high-quality scientists were also in high demand. How do you attract and keep such individuals in a very competitive environment? And how do you finance growth in that kind of milieu?

The answer to both was employee ownership. The company grew rapidly in its early years. From an initial revenue base of about a quarter of a million dollars, within four years revenues had reached $10 million, and within a decade climbed to over $100 million. This growth could have been financed through external stock offerings, but that could have meant tying it to the short-term pressures of quarterly financial performance, something Beyster saw as incompatible with the goal of long-term stability. Employee ownership, however, put questions of the company's interests in the hands of those who had the largest stake in the answer, and in the process established a rewards system that was fundamentally fair.

Currently we have about nineteen thousand shareholders, with our employees owning the bulk of the stock. We're proud of this. The employee ownership we've built attracts and retains the very best people. And that's a very smart investment.

## Coping with Centrifugal Forces and Niches

We believe decentralized decision making in an organizational structure that pushes authority downward has a number of advantages. It has some potential dangers, too. The most obvious one—probably noted in every business text on corporate management written in the last hundred years—is the centrifugal orientation in decentralized organizations that tends to push profit centers into niches.

This can be a beneficial pattern, particularly if you believe finding niches in today's markets is the highway to profit. Collectively, it turns out to be a form of corporate expansion that limits strategic risks. That is, you can think of the various profit centers in a decentralized business structure as dynamic pursuers of opportunity. And because the amount of resources they control are less than the bulk of corporation assets, the effects of wrong choices, poor strategic planning, and other mistakes on the part of the profit centers are limited. The financial health of the corporation is not threatened directly because of errors in judgment or planning by individual profit centers.

Most organizational experts recognize, however, that it's relatively easy for decentralization to prompt turf concerns and internal corporate competition. A business entity that has developed a niche wants to protect it. It has usually been secured with a lot of effort, for those who occupy business niches in the marketplace have to demonstrate they should be the niche provider. But with a niche secured, it's a lot easier to think outside the niche—to hunt for other niches. And that, of course, leads to intracorporate competition, both in the form of trying to keep other corporate profit centers off the secured turf and in the form of poaching on another's turf.

Now, we ought not to be too critical of intracorporate competition. It's a form of entrepreneurial activity, after all, and whether the competition comes from inside or outside the corporation, competition for markets has some general benefits to clients, the larger society, and the economy. And it has benefits to the corporation, enlivening its components, stimulating agility, and making things interesting.

The real problem with intracorporate competition has to do with the accoutrements that sometime accompany it. The ones we watch carefully involve transparency and whether "nicheism"— which ultimately involves being very good at solving very narrow problems—undermines our ability to work together. So the issue is how to keep niches from working against the core values of the corporation and its long-term financial health. It's not a question of right or wrong, but of proper balance.

SAIC does not encourage mindless risk taking, and we don't reward mistakes or pay the profit centers that make them. Although a decentralized organization buffers the financial cost of individual profit center errors, those errors hurt the corporation's reputation. And a tarnished corporate reputation hurts everyone in the corporation—in their pocketbooks—because it's owned by the employees.

What I've just sketched, of course, is one of the cultural benefits of a wholly employee-owned corporation. Employee ownership imposes a kind of corporate conscience on everyone that simply does not exist in other corporate forms. That's a very important dynamic governor. It doesn't slow or prevent the centrifugal patterns of business activity associated with decentralized organizations, but keeps some of the dangers inherent in such organizations in check. It's not really a procedure or a structural factor so much as a cultural phenomenon.

## Information Flows and Synergy

There are a couple of other techniques or procedures we use to keep a healthy balance. One is something we call "meetings week." Held once every three months, meetings week is committed largely to showcase and make transparent what the individual profit centers are doing. The goal is not to check up on what is underway or to challenge it. It's to make it visible so that others having similar projects or insights can begin to share views and experiences. In short, it is a consciously designed technique devoted to balancing specialization with potential synergism.

We've found that meeting every quarter is about right in terms of frequency. It's high enough to keep in touch with projects and low enough to see changes in the projects. We fill in-between weeks with a lot of communications across profit centers, facilitated by a corporate e-mail system and additional meetings.

And we use financial resources to reward synergy. The key to gaining financial compensation in SAIC is to be innovative in bringing together different capabilities of the company. That's our corporate forte to the external world, and it's the backbone of synergism inside the company. So we reward those inside the company who do so. The rewards take several forms, including the traditional ones of promotions and salary increases, and those that employee ownership makes possible, such as rewards of stock and stock options.

I'd like to describe a fourth technique. It's a relatively new process that we're testing for utility. It's called the "SAIC global issues project" and it centers on about ten big problems. These are truly big problems, so broad and often so intractable that it's perhaps pretentious to lay them out and use them as a vehicle for balancing the centrifugal tendencies in a decentralized organization.

For example, problems such as disease, energy, water, and governance are on our list, stated in just that very general way.

Why use such broad categories? It's a conscious choice. We wanted to start with issues so broadly framed that, at the entry level of discussion, there are no wrong views or suggestions. There's a natural tendency to take issues and deal with them in an Aristotelian manner; that is, to break them into their component parts and solve the parts. It's a very bureaucratic approach that revolves around the effort to send parts of a problem to those parts of the organization that have experience in dealing with similar issues. And it's not a bad approach, particularly in centralized, hierarchical organizations where the broader solutions are assembled as the component parts move up the hierarchy.

But the Aristotelian approach doesn't work too well in decentralized organizations. There, it simply reinforces nicheism, for each of the profit centers tend to select those aspects of an issue they have the most familiarity with and to apply solutions that worked in the past on similar problems. That's not a good recipe for generating synergy. Decentralized organizations lack the hierarchy that ostensibly helps pull parts of a solution together, so you need other mechanisms.

That's one reason we've found it helpful to build dialogues, discussions, and interchanges inside SAIC around these very broad problems. Something like disease or energy is so broad that it's not easy to pigeonhole into niches. But those with such niches can often find broad issues interesting in terms of how their niche might help come to a more general solution to a very broad problem. And a discussion that revolves around broad issues turns out to be more conducive to niche bridging than those that are less broad.

In any case, so far we've found the global issues project useful in getting the kind of systems integration and innovation that has great payoff potential, in getting various parts of SAIC talking with each other. Perhaps most importantly, it reinforces a foundation tenet of the company; namely, that we in SAIC work on problems that are worth solving.

## A Company Built for the Future

SAIC is a company fit for the times and for the future. In an Information Revolution, where a massive paradigm shift is occurring in a relatively short period, businesses that are the most flexible, agile, and responsive are the ones that will grow, profit, and expand. SAIC is such a company. Able to quickly assemble the resources and different perspectives of individual scientific teams, SAIC offers a sophisticated maturity for solving society's most complex problems. Our business is part of the Information Revolution, and we intend to keep riding that tiger with the skill, agility, wisdom, and quickness it demands.

# Conclusion

# Through the Eye of a Needle
## *The Coming Three Revolutions*

## William E. Halal

Now that you've read what my eighteen colleagues have to say,
let's review what has been learned. Think of this as a study.
By bringing together the best knowledge from a variety of leaders
in diverse fields, I hope to integrate all this information into a
coherent whole, a strategic scenario that helps us grasp the critical
changes needed in the next few years.

These chapters do not comprise a scientifically selected sample,
but the case for confidence is pretty good. It should be clear that
these people represent a broad spectrum of views: chief executives
in different industries, prominent scholars whose work is respected,
and seasoned consultants, all chosen to fill out the range of opinion.
The only bias they may be guilty of is that they tend to be inventive,
far-thinking, and generally progressive. But that is exactly why I
chose them—to provide insights that not everyone can summon.

## What Have We Learned?

Table C.1 summarizes the key points made in these chapters so that
we may gain a sound grasp of broad patterns in the data. By scanning across the concepts of different authors, we can see if their
ideas support or refute the three principles of the introductory chapter, gain a more realistic appreciation for how these principles work
in practice, and elaborate finer points.

**Table C.1. Summary of Concepts**

| Chapter | Enterprise | Cooperation | Knowledge |
|---|---|---|---|
| Goldsmith, Indianapolis | Governments compete<br>Units must compete | Internal and external cooperation also essential | Rewards must be based on performance |
| Ackoff | Transformation needed to an internal market | Internal markets form a sound basis for cooperation | Internal markets aid performance evaluation |
| Starr, Alcoa | Self-support creates healthy business units | Cooperation within self-directed units | Internal markets require new financial systems |
| Gable, Koch | MBM replicates an external economy | MBM creates more productive relationships | MBM creates knowledge |
| Lehrer, Lufthansa | Internal market needed<br>Managers like freedom & rewards | Leadership<br>Culture<br>Networking | Transfer prices cause problems<br>Going global |
| Taylor, MCI | Constant change<br>Multidisciplinary teams/units<br>Decentralize | Alliances are essential | IT networks<br>Knowledge companies<br>Global IT system |
| Miles | Technological change<br>Cellular units<br>Networks | Network of alliances<br>Interorganizational teamwork | Spherical organization<br>Training<br>Share knowledge |
| Lipnack & Stamps | Independence<br>Multiple leaders | Integration<br>Voluntary links | Unifying purpose |

| | | | |
|---|---|---|---|
| Holbrooke, Novell | Constant change<br>Organic units | Networking<br>No ownership | Share knowledge |
| Oklewizc, Telepad | Constant change<br>Customer service<br>Speed to market | Temporary vs. permanent alliances<br>Manage conflict | Shared knowledge<br>Shared vision |
| Smith, Bell Atlantic | Constant change | Alliances | Global IT network<br>Virtual offices<br>Knowledge society |
| Walters, Oklahoma | Change is coming<br>Decentralize<br>Pay-for-performance | Alliances<br>Networking | Virtual office<br>Training |
| Malone | Constant change<br>Customer demands<br>Decentralize<br>Customize | Alliances<br>Trust | Global IT network<br>Virtual alliances<br>Smart products |
| Pinchots | Intraprise<br>Choice<br>Intracapital | Community<br>Equality<br>Legal system | Vision<br>Free flow of information<br>Learning |
| Kuperman, Chiat/Day | Constant change<br>Customer service<br>Open building | Cooperate with all stakeholders | Virtual office<br>IT networks |
| Owens, SAIC | Decentralization<br>Autonomous units | Employee ownership<br>Common meetings | Global issues |

Looking over entries in the first column, it seems clear that constant change and other forms of turbulence demand ever more creative, responsive forms of internal enterprise. Steve Goldsmith, Russell Ackoff, the cases of Alcoa, Lufthansa, Koch, SAIC, and most other chapters consistently call for decentralized structures, self-supporting units, entrepreneurial freedom, internal competition, and accountability to clients. Mayor Goldsmith provides a keen summary of this view:

> As we search for more effective ways to organize life in the Information Age, one of the first things we should do is to break up large, unresponsive, monopolistic governments. . . . I have learned that nothing improves government more than the introduction of competition.

Scanning the second column leads to much the same conclusion about cooperation. Almost all chapters, especially those of Jerry Taylor at MCI, Ray Miles, Lipnack and Stamps, and the cases of Novell and Telepad highlight the virtues of teamwork, networking among internal units, collaborative alliances, and corporate communities. Jerry Taylor explains how cooperation creates value out of diverse interests:

> No company has all the needed capital, resources, talent, or products to compete across all geographies and industries. Competing globally means one thing: forging alliances, joint ventures, and partnerships. The most crucial requirement is to ensure that each partner brings something of value to the relationship. The strength of an alliance is measured by the net economic value it creates.

Finally, the third column confirms the imperative for using knowledge. The reason and form it takes may vary, from global information networks to performance measures, employee training, virtual organizations, strategic direction, or an inspiring vision. But Ray Smith of Bell Atlantic, David Walters, the Pinchots, Bob Kuperman at Chiat/Day, Terri Holbrooke at Novell, and others agree that knowledge offers possibilities that are boundless. Ray Smith provides the rationale:

> In the Industrial Age, wealth derived from raw materials, size, and other physical attributes. In the Information Age, wealth is a function of information, vision, and other properties of the mind. Unlike raw materials, knowledge can't be used up. The more of it you dispense, the more you generate. Economics used to be ruled by the law of diminishing returns. Now we can enjoy expanding returns.

Such statements from leading CEOs, scholars, and consultants, along with the many examples and data reported here, show that the principles needed to transform organizations are at hand. When the mayor of a major city proposes introducing competition into his government, the need for internal enterprise systems is manifestly clear. If the CEO of what is possibly the toughest company in the toughest industry professes the virtues of working together productively, who can argue? And when the CEO of a rapidly growing corporation explains how to realize the infinite power of knowledge, we should listen.

Enterprise, cooperation, and knowledge are the central principles that increasingly govern organizations. These ideas are still rather novel, and so they are often not understood, hard to implement, or resisted for personal reasons. But managers will have to think and behave along these lines because it is increasingly necessary to do so.

Organizations will soon be routinely designed and managed as constantly shifting clusters of internal enterprise units, possibly from the CEO's office down to the grassroots of self-managing teams.

They will be connected together by interactive information networks into a dense web of alliances, including close working relationships between employees, customers, suppliers, competitors, and governments to form a seamless global economy. And this entire economic infrastructure will focus its energies on the pursuit of knowledge to advance social progress.

## The Coming Economic Reversal

Let me play devil's advocate at this point by raising the many doubts and objections to this scenario that probably dwell on the minds of most people.

### Why Should We Adopt These Changes?

At the time of this writing, Americans were feeling good about the economy. Companies were thriving on a major economic boom, the Dow Jones average soared past 8,000 and seemed headed for 10,000, while both inflation and unemployment remain low. As 1997 began to unfold, a *Washington Post* headline story announced: "The economy appears to have entered a new period of stability in which recessions no longer seem inevitable."[1]

Why, then, should managers struggle to adopt these draconian measures, Professor Halal? If we just let the marketplace do its work, companies will remain competitive without all these dramatically different and very uncertain changes you propose. CEOs will never relinquish their power, nor should they if we hope to maintain an orderly world. It's naive to think that we should just transform organizations into some chaotic type of enterprise system, cooperate with everyone in sight, and use knowledge to improve the social welfare.

### The Old Rules No Longer Apply

The same objections have always been raised over the prospect of major change. Who would have believed that communism would just collapse? That the U.S. government would "reinvent" itself?

That the most powerful corporations would enter decline and be forced to restructure, reengineer, and reform?

The message my colleagues and I want to stress is that the world is entering such an uncharted new frontier, an epoch so fundamentally different that the old rules no longer apply. The conventional wisdom of the past must be replaced by concepts that conform with the new realities of infinite knowledge:

- Order can be best achieved—not through control and planning—but through entrepreneurial freedom.

- Strength comes—not out of power and firmness—but through cooperative community.

- Abundance flows out of—not material riches—but a subtle frontier of boundless understanding, meaning, and spirit.

These are not simply theories, they are descriptions of leading practice that represent the primary source of economic power today, principles as hard and ruthless as the principles of gravity and of biological life and death. These forces of change should be especially severe because a sharp look at a few major trends quickly reveals that a massive upheaval looms ahead.

## The Coming Tenfold Leap in Growth

Americans may be leading the world economically, but isn't this largely a short-term result of retrenchment rather than productive growth? Stephen Roach, chief economist at Morgan Stanley, called it the "hollow ring of the productivity revival," and Jim Stanford, CEO of Petro-Canada, said, "You can't shrink to greatness." Today's management will prove no match for the sophisticated technologies that should arrive about the end of this decade. Andy Grove of Intel put it best: "The Internet is like a tidal wave, and we are in kayaks."[2]

Can it be only a few years since the Internet became the de facto communications network for a new global order? The Internet has been accepted by roughly fifty million people and five hundred thousand companies around the world, and intranets and extranets have become the standard for organizational communications. As Jerry Taylor and Ray Smith pointed out, growth is projected to reach 250 million people by 2000—still covering only a few percent of its potential as the world's primary communication service.

The same exponential growth is expected for telephones, television, wireless, and other communication technologies. Satellites now beam TV coverage to 1.2 billion people on every continent, and will soon reach most of the other 4.5 billion. Wireless service for voice, fax, data, and video is growing 50 percent per year and should span the majority of people in industrialized nations and many in developing nations by 2000.

Even more revolutionary technologies lie right around the corner. Dell Computer has figured out how to sell $1 million worth of PCs over the Internet per day. Several ventures are underway to launch hundreds of satellites that will provide an "Internet in the sky" for anyone around the world. Webcasting, Java applets, intelligent agents, virtual communities, the video PC, and other paradigm-breaking innovations are sure to follow.

These trends paint a bold but realistic scenario for about 2000–2005 A.D. when all social and economic activities may be conducted electronically. The typical home or office will likely be connected into a worldwide system where people can shop, work, bank, play, learn, and even worship over interactive multimedia networks. The richness of this system should combine the intelligence of a computer, the communications of the telephone, and the vivid reality of television. Rather than hunching over a keyboard, we may use voice commands to write documents, make phone calls, hold video conferences, and watch movies and TV images—all projected on wall monitors with life-size images.

As these advanced technologies move capital, knowledge, technology, and even labor swiftly around the world seeking their highest returns, a brushfire of competition is roaring over governments, corporations, and individuals everywhere. The place where this revolution began highlights the change. In 1996, when London celebrated the tenth anniversary of its "Big Bang" that deregulated British financial markets, England had the highest level of capital investment, the most robust economic growth, and the lowest unemployment levels in the European Union.[3]

From London, to Moscow, to Tokyo, to Beijing, to Rio, to Washington, D.C., politicians and CEOs now grasp the main message: free markets draw investment, promote entrepreneurship, employ skilled labor, encourage growth, and improve the lives of people. Even Parisian storekeepers and waiters now accept the reality that they must smile and be pleasant to attract customers.

To top it off, this raging process of globalization is likely to increase economic growth tenfold. Apart from the satiated West, most of the world is starved for the same material comforts now enjoyed by a few prosperous nations. Moreover, the number of people in undeveloped nations is five times that in developed nations, and they are almost certain to double as they industrialize. Thus, the stark reality is that all of today's major crises are likely to increase by roughly a factor of ten over the long term.

Specifically, the level of industrial production, international competition, change and innovation, demand for scarce resources, environmental degradation, and cultural diversity will all grow roughly tenfold. The industrialization of China alone should at least double these crises, and India will double them again.[4]

Thus the world faces the unprecedented challenge of creating a new system of political economy that can manage such a leap in growth on a planet already suffering from congestion, conflict, scarcity, environmental stress, and complexity. To believe that an extension of our present system will somehow muddle through is wishful thinking.

## The Crisis of Maturity

The great scientist, science fiction author, and futurist Arthur C. Clarke studied obstacles to change: the countless experts who always seem to insist that all the great advances of history were impossible, such as those who objected that man would never fly. Clarke found that the evidence needed to forecast these historic turning points was always available and the revolutionary impact was well understood. The problem was a failure of imagination and nerve—the inability of smart people to fathom the strong likelihood that the world will soon behave very differently, and their lack of courage to acknowledge what they suspected.[5]

Managers of almost all institutions are failing to lead because they suffer from this same failure of imagination and nerve pointed out by Clarke. Most of what passes for informed debate and leadership today is simply out of touch with this huge challenge that looms dead ahead. The evidence is all about us, yet leaders usually seem to think all that's needed are marginal changes—even as the structures of today's outmoded institutions are trembling with the approach of a social earthquake.

It could be thought of as a "crisis of maturity." People in all nations must learn to manage the inevitable transition to a technological world of unfathomable complexity and change. We will have to create sophisticated organizational metastructures, decentralize control to ordinary people, design international knowledge networks, resolve differences with our adversaries, develop modest but adequate lifestyles, cultivate our wisdom, and pray for spiritual unity. In short, we have to grow up and behave as responsible adults—there is no alternative.

Russell Ackoff, Michael Malone, and my other coauthors think this is nothing less than a complete social transformation, and Gary Hamel proposes that corporate strategy should be "subversive of the status quo."[6] Robert Shapiro, CEO of Monsanto, echoes the inevitability of this historic change: "No demographer questions that the population will double around 2030. Without radical change, the kind of world implied by those numbers is unthinkable. The whole system has to change; there's a huge opportunity for reinvention."[7]

This challenge is highlighted by seeing how the three principles of progress are each driving a major "economic reversal" as we pass through this transformation—they can be thought of as revolutions.

## The Revolution from Control to Freedom

If we hope to create dynamic organizations able to master a tenfold increase in complexity that looms ahead as far as the eye can see, it will be necessary to extend free enterprise beyond anything that now exists. Today's flexible hierarchies will prove no match for the revolutionary technologies, sophisticated products, demanding customers, bright young employees, diverse markets, and hypercompetition now appearing around the globe.

A flood of authorities constantly worries over this need to cope with constant, turbulent change: "Organizations of the 21st Century will be constantly reconfiguring because change is happening all the time"; "Organizations everywhere are starting to compete on their ability to change faster and more effectively than their rivals"; "The perfect company today is almost structureless. All that holds it together is its culture."[8]

Within this context, most organizations look as primitive as the old Soviet economy. Consider IBM, a focal point of corporate America. Lou Gerstner seems to have saved Big Blue from the financial abyss and raised its stock price dramatically, but the value of its individual divisions totaled $115 billion in 1996 while the parent company's stock was valued at $65 billion. The lost $50 billion represents wealth that has been destroyed by IBM's corporate management. Managers claim the software division alone wastes $200 million each year getting headquarters approval of its ten thousand software projects.[9]

Rather than really using IBM's vast wealth of knowledge and creative people to pioneer the IT frontier, Gerstner's main contribution seems to consist of imposing discipline: firing half the workforce, slashing costs and debt, and refocusing marketing efforts on IBM's old corporate customers. Here's how IBM managers describe their new boss: "His blunt style sent tremors through the organization"; "If you expect to be stroked, forget it"; "He is terribly concerned about stature, particularly his own."[10]

Hierarchical control may still pass for leadership in such situations, but—like painting over rotted timbers—it merely masks the underlying weakness and invites catastrophe. How long can an aging Big Blue withstand the relentless advances of countless other computer makers? Competitors such as Dell Computer are applying their low-cost, on-line strategy to large machines, and even China is becoming a player.[11]

The real solution is a fundamentally different approach to management that harnesses the creative talents lying dormant in average people. As Fortune 500 dinosaurs downsized by three million employees during the past decade, smaller firms and new ventures upsized by creating twenty-one million new jobs.[12]

TQM, reengineering, and other popular practices are useful, but the main need is to shift the locus of power from top to bottom, to think of management in terms of enterprise rather than hierarchical control. I know this sounds revolutionary, but this *is* a revolution—an Information Revolution—that is at least as dramatic as the Industrial Revolution. Just as the idea that communism might yield to markets seemed preposterous only a few years ago, a similar restructuring seems to be coming in large corporations—a "corporate perestroika."

One sign of this impending change can be seen in the devolution of power, responsibility, and rewards to operating levels. Performance-based pay for self-managed teams and business units has been growing steadily and is now beginning to seriously alter the relationship with corporate management. Here's how the trend is seen by the Hay Group, America's largest consulting firm in compensation: "Companies are putting more and more compensation on the variable side, as opposed to fixed salary, and they're weighting it more heavily to performance."[13]

It only takes a little imagination to extend these trends to the point where the logic of enterprise rules rather than the logic of hierarchy. If we could recognize that economic value is created at the operating level, and that most modern employees are better able to manage their own affairs than CEOs are, the way ahead becomes clear. Corporate executives should relinquish direct control by creating internal enterprises of all operating units down to the level of work teams. Listen to how Robert Shapiro of Monsanto describes this solution to the radical change he warned of a few pages ago: "We have to figure out how to organize [employees] in ways that enable them to coordinate their work without wasteful and intrusive systems of control. People give more if they control themselves."[14]

As Bill Owens of SAIC shows in his chapter, this does not mean that CEOs give up power. They design these organizational structures and provide leadership to unify units into a cooperative, strategically guided system. This pivotal change would also resolve today's nagging issues of downsizing, reengineering, quality, and the like by placing the responsibility for them on self-managed teams that are accountable for the use of resources to serve clients profitably. In this capacity, CEOs may be more influential because they would be leading a system in which everyone shares the responsibility for success.

## The Revolution From Conflict to Community

We saw throughout other chapters the growth of cooperation among internal units, suppliers, distributors, and partners, and how this same collaboration is being extended to employees, customers, government, and other stakeholders. This trend leads to an interesting paradox that pulls organizations in opposing directions: complexity demands entrepreneurial freedom, but there is an equally compelling need for a second revolution that unifies this diversity into a coherent, productive whole.

Although cooperation is productive, any relationship is likely to change with shifts in technology, markets, and clients. So managers must build trusting partnerships that form a community of common values and purpose—while acknowledging that this is a fluid, dynamic community of changing members. This polarity has always existed but it is reaching new heights as competition demands higher performance of more complex organizations.

An entirely different business culture is evolving that recognizes the need for change and even celebrates it as a natural part of life—rather like the way students enter college and then leave with fond memories of their alma mater. Corporations increasingly resemble universities in a Knowledge Society, so some similar ethic is needed. Ron Oklewizc of Telepad suggests in his chapter that managers should not think of "marrying" partners but simply "dating" or "going steady."

The problem is that cooperation and community run counter to the ideology of capitalism. Americans in particular are dedicated to the idea that corporations are owned by shareholders and so their goal should be to maximize profits.

Business must be profitable, but this view places managers in the difficult posture of opposing the interests of their employees, customers, and others whose support is essential. Employee pay and training, for instance, are then viewed as simply costs to be avoided. But companies such as Marriott and Motorola, which have formed employee partnerships, enjoy returns of several hundred percent on their investments in training.[15]

This business-society conflict has everyone confused, wasting energy rather than working together toward common goals. Robert Haas, CEO of Levi Strauss, explained the problem: "People look through the wrong end of the telescope, as if profits drive business. Employee morale, turnover, consumer satisfaction . . . that's what drives financial results."[16]

Let's look more closely at the issue of downsizing, an icon symbolizing this crisis of capitalism. The famous case of Al Dunlap is particularly revealing.[17] As CEO of Scott Paper, Dunlap did succeed in restructuring the firm so effectively that the company's stock rose 225 percent. That is an impressive achievement, for which he was rightly rewarded. But this is impressive mainly in terms of the capitalist ideology just noted. From the emerging view of corporate community, it looks very different:

> *Employees.* The CEO received $100 million for two years of work and other executives profited on the order of $10–20 million each. Yet 12,000 people lost their jobs, which so traumatized some that they suffered strokes and other serious illnesses. Later another 8,000 were fired when the firm was sold. What would one reasonably expect about morale, stress, and productivity?

> *Customers.* Sales fell because customers wondered about product quality and the company's ethics. Here's what one woman said: "Dunlap appears to be the embodiment of capitalism run amok—without heart, soul, or conscience. Whenever possible, I will use only the products of Scott's competitors."

> *Suppliers.* Dunlap scrapped the annual meeting with suppliers intended to improve working relations, raise quality, and lower prices. Despite the fact that almost all well-managed firms today are developing exactly this type of collaborative relationship with their suppliers, his logic was simply, "This is nonsense."

Little wonder that this case aroused such passions from fellow CEOs, scholars, journalists, and ordinary people, as shown in Box C.1. Peter Capelli of The Wharton School had this explanation: "Dunlap didn't create value. He redistributed income from the employees and the community to shareholders."

The irony is that there seems to be little redeeming purpose to such mindless pursuit of wealth. Earning millions does not make people happier, nor does it meet the need for social connection and meaning that we all struggle with ultimately. After his victory, Dunlap admitted feeling blue: "It was an empty feeling. There was a hollowness there, like part of me was gone." Not very surprising. When

---

**BOX C.1. OPINIONS ON DOWNSIZING**

*Robert Samuelson,* economic columnist, *Washington Post:* "It's morally irresponsible and unjustifiable for top executives to receive huge pay-checks while throwing people out the door."

*Max DePree,* former chairman and CEO, Herman Miller: "I can't recall any time in recent history where the anti-business rhetoric has been so strong."

*A middle manager in a downsized company:* "The cuts don't make strategic sense. We've gotten no salary increases, and now the CEO gets a large one. We set priorities on everything that needed to be cut, but did the executive dining room go? Did the corporate helicopter go? Who's kidding whom?"

*William May,* former chairman and CEO, American Can Company: "CEOs asked for it. They've been compensated at astronomical levels."

*Charles Heckscher,* chairman, labor studies and employment relations, Rutgers University: "We are in the middle of the biggest transition since the early years of this century. The lesson from the '30s is that a collapse of confidence can bring down the economic system."

*Sources:* "Backlash," *Across the Board* (July–Aug. 1996), pp. 24–29; "The Shredder," *Business Week* (Jan. 15, 1996), pp. 56–61; Letters to the Editor, *Business Week* (Feb. 5, 1996).

---

Al Dunlap meets his God in a few years, what can he offer on his behalf? That he made a lot of money for the shareholders?

No sum will make a whit of difference in such personal matters, and great wealth usually becomes a great burden. Bill Gates noted, "Giving away money effectively is almost as hard as earning it in the first place."[18] What does one do with more than a few hundred thousands dollars per year, much less the huge sums lavished on capitalist royalty such as Al Dunlap? Can Michael Ovitz really use the $90 million he got for leaving Disney? What could justify Michael

Milkin's $500 million income in one year? A 1994 survey revealed that 90 percent of Americans thought athletes, media stars, and CEOs are paid excessively.[19]

Those who perform well deserve special rewards, but it should be clear that America's adulation of wealth and material consumption has become a curse rather than a blessing. We have created a class of aristocrats who own so much money that it loses any meaning, while a third of the nation is so desperate that people hold two jobs, and some commit crimes, to survive. In short, the rich have become inhuman through their excesses, and the poor have been made subhuman by their poverty.

I suggest the solution lies in appreciating the crucial changes now being introduced by the Information Revolution. After a long history of zero-sum conflict, knowledge has altered the laws of economics to make cooperation efficient. Corporate community, then, is not social responsibility in the sense of doing good; it is a competitive advantage.

But our actions and beliefs have not yet caught up with this new reality. If working with employees, suppliers, customers, and even competitors is beneficial, it follows that the mission of business must somehow encompass all these interests instead of simply making profit for shareholders. Dan Mehan, AT&T's international vice president for quality and business management, summed it up this way in a personal conversation: "After the quality programs, reengineering, and other innovations are implemented, the final questions that count are: Will our customers continue to patronize us because they receive value? Will our employees be glad they joined and want to do their jobs well? Will the community accept us as good citizens? And last but certainly not least, will investors continue to see us as an attractive stock?"

The best way to resolve the perennial business-society conflict is to realize that modern enterprise should become a quasi-democratic institution that serves a changing community of stakeholders. As the many fine companies noted in this book demonstrate, both financial and social interests are not only perfectly compatible, they enhance one another.

The Japanese and Europeans have known this for decades, which is why they enjoy the highest overall quality of life in the world. My surveys show that the majority of managers now understand they must cooperate with their stakeholders and strive to serve their interests because trusting relationships are key to economic success. This is confirmed by other prominent evidence, such as Fortune's annual list of America's Most Admired Companies, which rates firms on scales that include employee benefits, customer service, and public goodwill.[20]

## The Revolution from Materialism to Spirit

The two previous revolutions, from control to freedom and from conflict to community, must be followed by a third revolution that may be the most daunting of all. A knowledge society makes no sense unless it embraces worthy purposes.

If modern business is to be viable, it has to do more than be productive, adaptable to change, collaborative, and knowledge seeking. It must also comprise a civilized economic system that represents a better way of life. It has to offer opportunities and security for everyone, both the skilled and the unskilled, those blessed with talents and those less fortunate. In short, it has to serve some worthy social purpose: producing valuable products and services, offering people meaningful lives, protecting the environment, and fostering a compatible global order. If it fails this test, resistance from government, labor unions, and other interests is certain.

A good example is the tobacco industry. Nicotine now imposes annual health care costs of $100 billion in addition to the four hundred thousand lives it cuts short every year in the United States—far more than all illegal drugs combined. But these companies have resisted attempts to curtail the health risks and they are now going global. A study by the Harvard School of Public Health found that smoking is the single biggest cause of disability and early death. "The tobacco epidemic is a global emergency," it said.[21] In economic terms, this industry destroys huge amounts of social value to make money for its investors. Is this a worthy pursuit for grown men and women? How long can it last?

Although I like the idea of social purpose, I do not argue it on moral grounds but because there is something mysterious about knowledge that requires it. Knowledge is a perishable commodity, a fluid that leaks through containing boundaries, and its value differs enormously under a variety of factors. Perhaps the biggest mystery is finding one's way through the growing avalanche of expanding information. It is ironic that having more data often leaves us more confused from the sheer limitlessness of it all. This mysterious quality makes information meaningless unless guided by values, vision, and purpose. That's why we see a rising interest in these qualities among organizations—including spirituality.

One of the most striking changes in the late 1990s is the way spirituality has erupted into popular attention. Look at the way politicians across the spectrum have rushed to embrace values and morality. In the two years after Thomas Moore published *Care of the Soul*, eight hundred books appeared with "soul" in their title.[22] Most surprising is the advent of a rapidly growing segment of American business people who proclaim spirituality as the central focus of their management philosophy.

Many CEOs, such as Ed McCraken of Silicon Graphics, make no bones about their practice of meditating daily. Hard-nosed engineering companies like EDS are realizing, "Technical knowledge is not a big deal anymore; the leaders who advance at EDS will be those who see the light." Now, EDS management teams start the day with a quiet period of reflection to soothing music so they can work together harmoniously with each other and their customers.[23]

This focus on purpose is badly needed to quell the constant flood of problems flowing directly from business's myopic focus on money. For instance, the health care industry recently outraged the nation by cutting costs rather heartlessly to improve profits. Predictably, Congress and most states are outlawing gag clauses that prohibit HMO physicians from telling patients about costly treatments, preventing

HMOs from forcing new mothers out of the hospital one day after delivery, and imposing other such regulations.

How did a great profession once dedicated to serving humanity get into such a mess? The answer seems rather easy: in an attempt to run today's notion of a good business, HMOs lost sight of their main purpose. We must all control costs, obviously, and investors must be rewarded if they are going to risk capital. But the final goal of business has to somehow serve society. If HMOs could look past the bottom line, they would find vast opportunities for serving unmet health needs.

Rather than simply treating illness, progressive health care systems *prevent* illness by helping people learn how to adopt healthier lifestyles, avoid harmful habits like smoking, prevent accidents, and other wellness measures. One HMO's staff visits patients to help them improve their living habits because it is far cheaper than paying for expensive operations later, thereby reducing costs while also improving health care. Jon Glaudemans, general manager of Aetna's Healthcare operations, agrees: "To achieve future cost savings, we must succeed in keeping patients healthy."[24]

Or take the case of the auto industry. Companies are struggling mightily to sell still more cars even as most cities around the world are chocked by congestion and pollution. Mexico City recently had a traffic jam that locked up all movement for two days. Britain and parts of the United States have halted building new roads, and *The Economist* recently called for bold measures to "tame the beast."[25]

We will always need cars, but the industry is challenged to redefine transportation needs. We could internalize environmental costs to discourage unnecessary driving, develop better public transportation, and use automated highway systems to control traffic wisely. There is great need for pollutant-free, low-energy, low-maintenance cars using some hybrid of fuel cells, solar energy, and flywheels. The gains for car owners, employees, and investors would revitalize the auto industry.

Almost every other industry and profession lends itself to a similar transformation, and many notable companies have demonstrated the power of adopting some worthy purpose. Anita Roddick transformed the cosmetics industry by serving the burgeoning need of people around the world for safe, inexpensive ways to care for their bodies while protecting nature. Skip Lefauve invented a human-centered enterprise by designing Saturn as self-managed teams of workers producing top-quality, inexpensive cars that are sold free of sales pressure.

If we could seriously reexamine all the myriad problems that abound today, we would see that they offer equally myriad opportunities for successful business. These abundant disorders can be insightfully reinterpreted as a vast frontier for a new type of enterprise, one that creates value out of working with various constituencies to serve everyone's needs better.

## Moving Through the Passage

If my eighteen coauthors and I are right, economies are passing through a complex set of three revolutions that is quietly gathering momentum. Exploding complexity is relentlessly decentralizing institutional controls, the benefits of collaboration are attracting diverse parties into pockets of corporate community, and knowledge invariably leads to a search for meaning and purpose. The increasing role women play at work, different attitudes of the young, and a general shift in values should also exert strong movement in this general direction.

Something like this is certainly needed. As free markets restructure the global economy, the comfortable safety nets of the welfare state are becoming torn by all this creative destruction, leaving people without the support of a civil society. The disparity of incomes between the top and bottom classes in the United States has returned to the levels reached prior to the Great Crash, exceeding all other industrialized nations. Overall, indices of social well-being have fallen to new lows.[26]

The result is predictable. At a 1996 meeting of the World Economic Forum in Switzerland attended by 1,200 CEOs and politicians, William Bennett, Secretary of Education under President Bush, and Rosabeth Moss Kanter, professor of business at Harvard University, cautioned that the loss of public support is causing a "backlash against capitalism." Even George Soros—perhaps the most famous capitalist of our time—issued a warning in an article titled "The Capitalist Threat."[27]

One of the greatest challenges the world will face in the years ahead is to bridge this chasm between the economic benefits of markets and the social needs of a civil society. The 1997 elections of socialist leaders in France and the Labor Party in Britain highlight the problem. Journalist E. J. Dionne wrote that the elections "redefine the terms of debate today by insisting there is more than one way to organize the global economy."[28]

Europeans, Japanese, and almost all other nationalities know they must encourage free markets to gain economic growth. "We are falling further behind in the race to stay competitive in a global economy," said a German politician. But they also accept the fact that they cannot abandon their citizens to the randomness of markets. A German business executive said, "We understand that poverty and other social ills are morally unacceptable and economically harmful." Norio Ohga, CEO of Sony, agrees: "We simply cannot fire people. It would only worsen the economy, and we really can't afford that." [29]

The only way I can imagine this conflict being resolved is by *moving through the passage*—by using the potential of this approaching economic reversal. The key is to see that free enterprise is not necessarily capitalism. As we've shown throughout this book, the fact is that enterprise is no longer powered primarily by capital—it is powered by knowledge.

Accepting this pivotal step then opens the path to a new system of political economy appropriate for a knowledge-based global order—the model we've outlined, in which small self-managed enterprises form pockets of corporate community, all guided by knowledge to serve worthy purposes. Britain's Prime Minister Blair proposed this same synthesis of the right and left: "Free markets and social welfare are not incompatible."[30]

Corporate executives are the primary candidates for creating this system because business is the most powerful institution in modern society. If they can accept a broader definition of their mission, corporations could become the central actors in this passage to maturity. Managers and CEOs could then shed their roles as the bad guys and assume their rightful place as heroes, the central leaders who help make the Knowledge Society work.

Surmounting this challenge will prove daunting, but it should also be an exciting adventure in creative enterprise. Unlike so much of the humdrum work of life, this is a once-in-a-lifetime opportunity to redefine our work roles, how institutions and economies are organized, even the purpose of life itself. Beyond product cycles and planning horizons, managing the transition to a world of infinite knowledge is a task managers must take seriously today.

One crucial, symbolic action would signify this institutional revolution, help us grasp it, and live up to it. Americans should stop calling our economic system "capitalism." I know we prize free markets, but capitalism is only one type of market system dedicated to the pursuit of capital, profit, and the other material factors that worked in the industrial past. If we want to draw on the energy of the future, we should define our economic system in terms of the resources of the future—the power of enterprise, community, and knowledge. I suggest a more accurate, fitting name would be "democratic enterprise."

Events are almost certain to surprise us, and so I wonder if we appreciate the difficulties ahead. Industrial Age values and systems may yield to their Information Age equivalent, but there is still no free lunch. The price for these gains is that organizational life is likely to resemble that great icon of IT, the Internet—dynamic and bursting with interconnected energy, but wild, untamed, and slightly out of control. Please also remember that an abstract world of knowledge is controversial, elusive, and raises profound questions that each views differently. And don't expect utopia, because all this will be badly needed simply to contain a tenfold rise in disorder.

At some point soon, however, a critical mass will grasp the logic of this emerging world, bringing about a historic reversal from power to freedom, conflict to community, and materialism to spirit. My surveys show that most managers sense this shift is coming, and they think it will happen sometime during the period 2000–2005.[31] What had heretofore been considered hopelessly idealistic may then become a hard, practical reality. And should we need a push now and then, we can always count on the power of the Information Revolution to back us up.

This mysterious, unusually difficult, and bigger-than-life quality of the coming passage reminds me of that teaching in the Bible that we all know intimately but have a hard time living up to: "It is easier for a camel to pass through the eye of a needle than for a rich man to enter the kingdom of heaven." I think something of this sort is exactly what lies dead ahead. We are all going to be sorely tried in a crucible of crisis to transform ourselves and our institutions during the next few years. It should feel like passing through the biblical eye of a needle.

### Notes

1. John Berry, "U.S. Sails on Tranquil Economic Seas," *Washington Post* (Dec. 2, 1996).

2. Stephen Roach, "The Hollow Ring of the Productivity Revival," *Harvard Business Review* (Nov.–Dec. 1997). Grove is quoted in "A Conversation with the Lords of Wintel," *Fortune* (July 8, 1996).

3. Fred Barbash, "Stodgy Little England Turns Wheeler-Dealer," *Washington Post* (Nov. 18, 1996), p. A13.

4. See the "Bruntland Report," World Commission of Environment and Development, *Our Common Future* (New York: Oxford University Press, 1987); and Wuppertal Institute for Climate, Environment, and Energy, *Carnoules Declaration: The Factor Ten Club* (Wuppertal, Germany: Wuppertal Institute, 1994).

5. Arthur C. Clarke, *Profiles of the Future* (Austin, Tex.: Holt, Rinehart, and Winston, 1984).

6. Gary Hamel, "Strategy as Revolution," *Harvard Business Review* (July–Aug. 1996), pp. 69–82.

7. "Growth Through Global Sustainability," *Harvard Business Review* (Jan.–Feb. 1997).

8. "Just Thinking About Tomorrow," *CIO Magazine* (Mar. 15, 1997); Arun Maira and Peter Scott, *The Accelerating Organization* (Cambridge, Mass.: McGraw-Hill, 1997); John Micklewait and Adrian Woolridge, *The Witch Doctors: Making Sense of the Management Gurus* (New York: Times Books, 1996).

9. "Defending Big Blue," *Newsweek* (Sept. 30, 1996), p. 50.

10. Betsy Morris, "Big Blue," *Fortune* (Apr. 14, 1997).

11. "Going Toe to Toe with Big Blue," *Business Week* (Apr. 14, 1997).

12. Peter Lynch, "The Upsizing of America," *Wall Street Journal* (Sept. 20, 1996).

13. Peter Behr and David Segal, "Finding New Ways to Carve Up the Rewards," *Washington Post* (Aug. 16, 1996).

14. "Growth Through Global Sustainability," *Harvard Business Review* (Jan.–Feb. 1997).

15. Bruce Pasternack and others, "People Power and the New Economy," *Strategy & Business* (Second Quarter 1997), Issue 7.

16. "Levi's," *Fortune* (May 12, 1997).

17. "The Shredder," *Business Week* (Jan. 15, 1996), pp. 56–61.

18. James Glassman, "Tightfisted at the Top," *Washington Post* (Dec. 17, 1996), p. A23.

19. Richard Harwood, "An Invisible Hand at the Pay Window," *Washington Post* (Apr. 19, 1997).

20. William E. Halal, *The New Management* (San Francisco: Berrett-Koehler, 1996), p. 77; Frederick Reichheld, *The Loyalty Effect* (Cambridge: Harvard Business School, 1996).

21. Joseph Califano, "The Tobacco Talks," *Washington Post* (June 3, 1997).

22. Kenneth Woodward, "More Chicken Soup for Barnes & Noble," *Newsweek* (Jan. 13, 1997), p. 64.

23. David Kirkpatrick, "This Tough Guy Wants to Give You a Hug," *Fortune* (Oct. 14, 1996), pp. 170–178.

24. David Hilzenrath, "What's Left to Squeeze?" *Washington Post* (Sept. 30, 1996).

25. Jessica Matthews, "Cars, Cars, Cars," *Washington Post* (Sept. 30, 1996).

26. *1996 Index of Social Health* (Tarrytown, N.Y.: Fordham Grad Center, 1996).

27. Karen Pennar, "A Helping Hand," *Business Week* (Mar. 24, 1997). "A Continent at the Breaking Point," *Business Week* (Feb. 24, 1997).

28. E. J. Dionne, "A Little Less Lean, Considerably Less Mean," *Washington Post* (June 6, 1997).

29. William Drozdiak, "German Economy Lags," *Washington Post* (May 7, 1997); Brenyon Schendler, "Japan: Is it Changing?" *Fortune* (June 13, 1994).

30. Paula Dwyer, "Tony Blair's Labor Party," *Business Week* (Apr. 15, 1997).

31. William E. Halal, *The New Management* (San Francisco: Berrett-Koehler, 1996), p. 236.

# Index